"STILL
and Still Moving"

RESTLESSNESS:
GIFT AND CHALLENGE

MARY TIMOTHY PROKES, FSE

xulon
PRESS

"STILL
and Still Moving"

RESTLESSNESS: GIFT AND CHALLENGE
by Mary Timothy Prokes, FSE

Printed in the United States of America.

ISBN 9781498482820

www.xulonpress.com

CONTENTS

ACKNOWLEDGEMENTS

Heart-deep thanks to Mother Shaun Vergauwen, Mother Superior, and to the entire body of the Franciscan Sisters of the Eucharist for the blessing of time to prepare this book. In turn, gratitude to the Very Reverend Denis Robinson, OSB, President-Rector, and to the Community of Saint Meinrad Seminary and School of Theology, for impeccable hospitality during the time of writing. The book's title *"Still and Still Moving"* is a celebrated phrase from T. S. Eliot's poem "East Coker." Together with the cover's panoramic photo of eastern Ireland's countryside, it serves as metaphor of the positive restlessness surging through creation.

Sister Mary Timothy Prokes, FSE

INTRODUCTION

"Are we there yet?" It's the familiar cry of children from the back seat of the family car. After they tumble out of constricting car seats, run through Grandma's house to check on pets and favorite treats, there can be a wistful pause, an unspoken feeling that they haven't really *arrived* at the total fulfillment of their built-up anticipation. For adults, the questions and longing are more penetrating. It is St. Peter's ecstatic asking if the trio who witnessed the Transfiguration might build three tents for Jesus, Moses and Elijah. He didn't really know *what* to say, but didn't want the experience to end. "Coming down the mountain" from an ecstatic encounter or celebration leaves an emptiness that invites intensified desire for "what is not yet."

Why do people pay to be securely fastened into uncomfortable seats, then slowly pulled up a steep metal track in order to be plunged at high speed in a terrifying roller coaster ride? Not once, but again and again. Why did Icarus of ancient lore long for wings to fly close to the sun? Or, why does a skier deliberately poise at the top of a ski-jump and then launch into the rush of a free-fall? *Nothing is ever enough.* At the core of every person there is the longing for a positive answer to the question: "Is there still more?" We are born restless, never satisfied with the present moment– and this is a gift!

Why write a book on *restlessness*? Isn't it obvious that in this present time we are experiencing a *restiveness* that is eating away at the heart of faith, culture, the very meaning of humanity? For that very reason it is important to focus on the difference between positive restlessness and forms of restiveness that are destructive. An insatiable restlessness is inherent in the human heart, an impulse toward fulfillment in eternal love that exceeds human imagination and invention. Further, a marvelous restlessness pervades all that exists, all that moves toward an unknown moment when even the finest experiences of present existence will give way to "a new heaven and a new earth."

Restiveness, on the other hand, describes a disquiet that is fractious, that is *un*toward and resistant to the divine design for creation. Restiveness characterizes a desire to eliminate all boundaries, not to attain ultimate fulfillment in divine love, but in order to achieve power over whatever limits or restrains swift satisfaction, endless novelty and excitement. Restiveness foments the pursuit (apart from a divine Creator) of definitive scientific explanations for all that exists. Antonio Lopez writes that "Man treasures novelty because, as Ratzinger explains, it is 'a replacement for the loss of divine love's inexhaustible wonder (*surprise*).'"[1] Negative restlessness involves a perception of self and the world that is *disengaged from* both self and the world, says Lopez.

Never before have there been so many ways and means to assuage the longing for experiences that will intrigue and challenge. The term "bucket-list" is now part of our vocabulary. Travel writer Henry Wismayer says that he spends a lot of time contemplating why people "venture abroad." Awesome places, natural and man-made "have become lodestars for the restless mind,"[2] but the sense of awe is being eclipsed. Wismayer used the example of the 1896 film in which a locomotive was approaching the camera and people fled in fear from the auditorium, whereas "Now we watch *The Hobbit*, where 3D armies of orcs, trolls, and warmongering dwarfs appear utterly, compellingly alive, and shuffle out of the multiplex feeling lobotomized."[3] What's the answer? asks Wismayer. For

---

[1] Joseph Ratzinger (now Pope Emeritus Benedict XVI), *Look to Christ: Exercises in Faith, Hope, and Love,* trans. Robert Nowell, (New York: Crossroads, 1991), 74, cited in Antonio Lopez, "On Restlessness," *Communio,* Vol. 34 (Summer, 2007), 180.

[2] Henry Wismayer, "The Death of Awe in the Age of Awesome," https://human.parts/the-death-of-awe-in-the-age-of-awesome-846fc4569751. (accessed Apr. 30, 2016).

[3] Wismayer, "The Death of Awe."

some, he says, it is in pushing further. "As awe diminishes, peril becomes increasingly coveted." Adrenaline-junkies know "that moments are lived more fully when stood on the precipice."[4] One of his friends is a biker, cycling around the world. Wismayer asked his views on awe. It is still attainable said his friend, but it's what arrives "unannounced." Agreeing, Wismayer said that awe can be closer than we think. In a park recently, he came upon a wren perched on a conifer branch. "For ten minutes it stood on its twig, chest puffed-out but still barely bigger than my thumb. And as it sang its exquisite warble it occurred to me that this little creature, half a mile from home, was just about the most awesome thing I've ever seen."[5]

This book is written to evoke prayerful reflection and discussion on the gift of positive restlessness, distinguishing it from a disquieting restiveness that often reaches for genuine awe and mystery "in all the wrong places." This book begins with reflection on the entire physical universe that races and throbs with a restlessness that, thanks to science and technology, we can know with increasing accuracy – but especially as a created mystery we will never fully penetrate.

The human heart, as St. Augustine cried out in his well-known prayer, knows a restlessness of being created

---

[4] Wismayer, "The Death of Awe."

[5] Wismayer, "The Death of Awe."

toward God. Every person in the entire human family, from its beginning, is on pilgrimage, drawn toward fulfillment in the unfathomable love of Father, Son and Holy Spirit. It is essential then, to ask how Christ's Eucharistic presence accompanies humanity on this journey, and how contemporary science and technology often propose *restive* solutions for the heart-cry that can only be fulfilled in what Christ revealed at the Last Supper.

Restlessness is not a new issue for humanity. Today, however, it seems "trendy" to dismiss as obsolete the wisdom of thinkers, poets and mystics who lived prior to an age of *apps* and avatars. It is too easy to confuse what is holy hunger of the heart for union with divine Persons with the tawdry yen for novel excitement "*right now.*" The poet Francis Thompson knew both the dregs that never satisfied, and his enduring restlessness for God. The amazing realization of Thompson was that a restless divine love was "hounding" him.

I fled Him, down the nights and down the days;
I fled Him, down the arches of the years;
I fled Him, down the labyrinthine ways
Of my own mind; and in the midst of tears
I hid from Him.....
Adown Titanic glooms of chasmed fears,
From those strong Feet that followed, followed after.
But with unhurrying chase,

And unperturbed pace,
Deliberate speed, majestic instancy,
They beat – and a Voice beat
More instant than the Feet –
'All things betray thee, who betrayest Me.'[6]

---

[6] Francis Thompson, "The Hound of Heaven," *The Oxford Book of Mystical Verse*, Nicholson & Lee, eds, 1917, 239.

Chapter I

"Still And Still Moving": The Gift And Challenge Of Restlessness

Home is where one starts from. As we grow older
The world becomes stranger, the pattern more complicated
Of dead and living. Not the intense moment
Isolated, with no before and after,
But a lifetime burning in every moment.....
We must be still and still moving
Into another intensity
For a further union, a deeper communion...[7]

It is a mid-winter afternoon in Indiana, but out-side my window a flurry of burnt-orange-breasted robins chatter and swoop in and out of frigid dogwood

---

[7]   Thomas Stearns Eliot, "East Coker," *The Four Quartets* (London: Faber and Faber, 1944), 22-23.

tree branches. Each bird pauses briefly on a twig and then relentlessly repeats its flight across the campus circle. The robins embody instinctual activity that foretells mating, nesting and the continuity of robin-life through fledglings. In flashes of living orange on the winter landscape, the flock also is depicting analogically the *mystery, gift and challenge* of **restlessness** that pervades creation, including the human heart.

Philosophers and physicists, poets and saints grapple with the meaning of restlessness. **Why** are we restless? How does restlessness characterize life itself and permeate the entire creation? It is obvious that technological and cultural restlessness is visibly increasing, often causing violent eruptions among individuals and nations. Restlessness in itself is not a new phenomenon, of course. Across the millennia it has been memorably described by writers as varied as the Hebrew psalmists, Saint Augustine, T. S. Eliot, and Thomas Merton. Perhaps the most familiar expression of it is Augustine's prayerful cry: "[F]or you have made us for yourself, and our heart is restless until it rests in you."[8]

A number of common synonyms for restlessness can be found in thesauruses and dictionaries, including words such as movement, turmoil, transiency, discontentment, inquietude, turbulence, unsettledness, and uneasiness

---

[8]   Saint Augustine, *Confessions*, B. I, Part 1, trans. John K. Ryan (New York: Doubleday and Co., 1960), 43.

– or the phrase "never still or motionless." One might add that restlessness refers to constant interchanges among members of the created universe, and a *being impelled beyond a given point*. Fingers lightly drumming on a table-top, or the persistence of a familiar melody running through one's mind can indicate a surface kind of restlessness, but they are like wavelets lapping on a lakeshore – mere intimations of what moves in the deep.

How reach what gnaws quietly, deep-down, at a seeming satisfaction with things as they are? Does our restlessness differ in kind from those who have preceded us? Is restlessness a predominantly human characteristic or is it an essential trait of *all that exists*?

The title of this book and lines quoted from T. S. Eliot's poem "East Coker" at the beginning of this chapter express a basic truth that will be pondered throughout this book: *"We must be still and still moving / Into another intensity / For a further union / A deeper communion."* Eliot compresses the paradox into seven words: **we must be still and still moving**. He probably wrote better than he knew. Some see his poem as dark, echoing the year 1940 when war had erupted in Europe. But the insight that Eliot had accords with his earlier poem "Burnt Norton," which contains the lines:

Time present and time past
Are both perhaps present in time future

And time future contained in time past.....
At the still point of the turning world. Neither flesh nor
fleshless;
Neither from nor towards; at the still point, there the
dance is,
But neither arrest nor movement. And do not call it fixity,
Where past and future are gathered.....
Except for the point, the still point,
There would be no dance, and there is only the dance...[9]

This book deals with the paradox of "still and still
moving." It is intended to evoke a shared pondering, a
"praying and thinking together" of what it means to live
in Christ *now*, in our present restlessness. There is an evident increase in turmoil in many of the world's societies
and nations, often roiling with cruelty, violence, greed,
and a desperate attempt to "move on." For many, there is
a press simply to move on – anywhere. It is an apt moment
to ask: what is the relationship between *rest* and *restlessness*? "Rest" suggests peacefulness, stillness, tranquility,
and lack of movement. What have these to do with restlessness, to be "still and still moving"? These interrelated
questions touch all of our relationships: with the extensive universe, our planet earth, our world-neighbors, our
inner heart, future humanity – and most of all, the Persons

---

[9] Thomas Stearns Eliot, "Burnt Norton," *The Four Quartets*, 7 and 9.

of the Trinity, in whose perichoretic image and likeness we are created. Divine Persons are at once the forever still point of all that is, and Love unceasingly given and received in dynamic interpersonal relationship.

Historical periods have often been named as "ages" or "eras" that define their predominant characteristics. Over the past few centuries, the length of such designated "ages" has shortened. For example, while the "The Age of Enlightenment " spanned more than a hundred years, the mere decade of the "Roaring Twenties" was followed swiftly by historic periods remembered as "The Great Depression" of the 1930's, the World War II Period, and "the Atomic Age." Recently, year-clusters tend to merge: the "Information Age" mingles with the "Millennial Age." As Ray Kurzweil explains in *The Singularity is Near*, the *linear* marking of time and events has yielded to *exponential* change which means that:

> [H]uman progress is exponential (that is, it expands by repeatedly *multiplying* by a constant) rather than linear (that is, expanding by repeatedly *adding* a constant..... exponential growth is seductive, starting out slowly and virtually unnoticeably..... The future is widely misunderstood. Our forebears expected it to be pretty much like their present, which had been pretty much

like their past..... But the future will be far more surprising than most people realize, because few observers have truly internalized the implications of the fact that the rate of change itself is accelerating.[10]

In prior centuries, linear thinking served well for practical human needs. For example, one commentator explained linear thought this way: if we build one house a day, in thirty days we will have thirty houses; if we eat one chicken a day we will need thirty for a month's supply.[11] "Millennial" author, David D. Bernstein, on the other hand, speaking of exponential progress said: "The fast future is the world we are currently living in. In 1968, '2001: a Space Odyssey' imagined what the world would be like in the then far off year of 2001. Today we can't even conceive of what the world might look like in forty years, let alone what to do with that information. We can no longer envision the future, even if just for fun. The future is coming at us faster and faster, the rate of change is increasing and

---

[10] Ray Kurzweil, *The Singularity is Near: When Humans Transcend Biology* (New York: Penguin Books, 2005), 10-11.

[11] See "The Future is Coming Much Faster than we Think, Here's Why," in http://www.thatsreallypossible.com/exponential-growth/ (accessed Jan.17, 2016).

the amount of change that takes place in a given year is skyrocketing as well."[12]

Millions of children, teens, and adults finger their fast-phones as I write this, texting messages to distant recipients, or often, to another person in the same room. There is the desire to move faster and go farther. Shanghai's "magnetic levitation" train, for example, invites would-be riders to know the exhilaration of ground travel at 270 miles per hour. There is the human press to exceed Olympic records, defy the limits of gravity, and enhance the human mind beyond its natural limits.

How shall we name the present era when experience and change are becoming ever more condensed? I suggest that ours, a time of increased grappling with the ever ancient, ever fresh experience of restlessness can well be termed the "*Age of Restlessness*." To say that ours is a "Restless Age" may seem too tame, too domesticated. Yet, "*restless*" applies to a broad spectrum of stirrings: from unsettled tectonic plates beneath the earth's crust before an earthquake – to the human heart in its yearning for fulfillment. From the beginning, we are *created on journey* to an eternal destiny beyond the restless universe. Will eternal life be a cessation of restlessness, or, rather, its peaceful intensification?

---

[12] "In Conversation with David Bernstein, Author of Fast Future" in "Fast Future: How the Millennial Generation is Shaping Our World." http://davidbernstein.com/fast-future/ (accessed Jan. 17, 2016).

In our "Restless Age" the instinctual ancient pattern of robins in picturesque flight can coexist with the calculated patterns of physicists who direct subatomic particles at the near-speed of light through the Large Hadron Collider in Switzerland. Both patterns witness to the mystery, challenge and gift of restlessness.

It is evident that there are different kinds of restlessness: from the interstellar to the inter-heart; from the inane and the perverse to the sacredly mysterious. Persons seeking the guidance of the Holy Spirit in the contemporary world do well to question *why* we are so restless. To ponder it is to encounter mystery – not "mystery" understood as a problem to be solved, but as profound truth to be entered ever more deeply. Karl Rahner said of mystery that it is "the impenetrable which is already present and does not need to be fetched....therefore not something provisional which is one day to be done away with or which in fact could be non-mysterious. It is the propriety which always and necessarily characterizes God – and through him, us."[13] Mystery, then, is not simply a "still undisclosed unknown,"[14] awaiting scientific explanation, but a reality that perpetually exceeds the finest human genius and explanation.

---

[13] Karl Rahner, "On the Theology of the Incarnation," in *Theological Investigations IV*, trans. Kevin Smyth (Baltimore, MD: Helicon Press, 1966), 108.

[14] Karl Rahner, "On the Theology of the Incarnation," 108.

Ultimately, we *live in mystery.* Can you remember the time when you first experienced a longing for the truly mysterious? Sometimes, recognition of the human heart's restless *longing* for what is mystery only rises to *consciousness* much later in life than when it was first experienced. I can remember sitting beneath a cottonwood tree on our family farm when I was about four years old. I recall looking intently at the grove that formed an enclosure for our home. Several years of drought had thinned the leaves of elms, boxelders and cottonwoods, letting light pierce through, especially when breezes nudged the branches. Over and over I would wait for a moment of stillness when a solid mass of leaves would form so that I could no longer see through them. Over ensuing decades, that longing endures. Even now, a certain tranquility "comes" if I drive or walk through groves or enter forests that darken solidly against the sky. It took many years for me to realize that even *bodily*, there endured from childhood a longing for mystery and its Maker, for *a concrete image for truth so deep and dense that I could never "see through" it.*

Can you recognize your own image of innate yearning for mystery? In *The Canticle of Creatures: Symbols of Union, an Analysis of St. Francis of Assisi*, Eloi Leclerc says:

"Imagined or oneiric images of material things have their roots in the soul. We do not have to wait for Bachelard to learn that 'every landscape we love is a state of soul.'"[15]

It is from that perspective, from mystery, that I want to ponder the rapid growth of human restlessness characteristic of our time. There is a deep-down-restlessness in the stillest of things that invites exploration. In both its massive and its minute expressions, burgeoning restlessness is opening human experience in ways previously unknown. *How can being sensitive to this affect our relationships to a good creation, to one another, and to the Father, Son and Holy Spirit?* Although it is not a new question, new answers are being asked of us as we live into a future that is "coming faster than we think."

Before reflecting on specific experiences of the "Restless Era" within human life in the twenty-first century, it seems helpful to turn the lens of thought briefly to a realistic wide-angle view, to consider that "from the beginning" a loving Creator launched, *from nothing,* a material universe astonishingly vibrant, pulsing with relational purpose expressed in time, space, and speed.

To begin there (as Genesis does) is to recognize and appreciate that the extensive universe is not simply the domain of scientists and mathematicians, but the privileged milieu of all who are created in the image and likeness of

---

15   Eloi Leclerc, *The Canticle of Creatures: Symbols of Union, an Analysis of St. Francis of Assisi* (Chicago: Franciscan Herald Press, 1977), 6.

God and who wrestle with exponential change. Creaturely gratitude will assist the "tossing in our hearts" how restlessness is inherent in the physical universe and how scientific and technical endeavors now impact human existence ever more rapidly. What does this means in the light of the Incarnation, the Eucharist, and the destiny of the human person created in the image of the Blessed Trinity?

We have become accustomed to the use of astronomical numbers. *The word "trillion" slides off the tongue like a dust mote down a shaft of light.* Yet, we live immersed in a universe measured in humanly incomprehensible figures. Consider with fresh attentiveness some of the familiar ways of expressing distances, speeds, and time – not as facts memorized for information but as realities evoking a prayerful sense of awe.

RESTLESS FROM THE BEGINNING

The universe in its entirety has been divinely created *restless*. Scripture sings in various ways of a seemingly paradoxical creation. The *Elohist* account of creation in Genesis, for example, opens with the elegant proclamation: "In the beginning God created the heavens and the earth. The earth was without form and void, and darkness was upon the face of the deep; and the Spirit of God was moving over the face of the waters."[16] In contrast, the author of I Samuel 2:8 stresses that there is an enduring stability of the earth: "For the pillars of the earth are the Lord's, and on them he has set the world." People in the time of Samuel could observe in the stability of stone pillars an apt explanation for their experience of the earth as secure and firm beneath their feet. How long it took to devise the instruments that probe beneath earth's skin and partially detect the realities that move deeply there! Metaphorically, the two accounts speak of "Still and still moving."

The elegant accounts of creation in Genesis are concise. Scientists are also spare in summarizing their findings concerning the act that initiated the material universe. Briefly, it was the "Big Bang." They attribute the bluntly-named massive explosion to the existence of a "particle" that provided the necessary *mass* needed for this to occur. The finest scientific tools and equipment have been used to search for a specific sub-atomic particle that caused the Big Bang:

> The 'God particle' is the nickname of a subatomic particle called the Higgs boson. In layman's terms, different subatomic

---

16 Genesis 1:1-2 in *The Holy Bible: Containing the Old and New Testaments*, Revised Standard Version, Catholic Edition (San Francisco: Ignatius Press, 1966). See footnote "b", p.1, that gives an alternative for "Spirit" as "wind." Unless indicated otherwise, all Scriptural references in this book are from this version.

particles are responsible for giving matter different properties. One of the most mysterious and important properties is mass. Some particles like protons and neutrons, have mass. Others, like photons, do not. The Higgs boson, or 'God particle,' is believed to be the particle that gives mass to matter. The 'God particle' nickname grew out of the long, drawn-out struggles of physicists to find this elusive piece of the cosmic puzzle..... As with any scientific discovery, God's amazing creation becomes more and more impressive as we learn more about it.[17]

On July 4, 2012, ATLAS and CMS announced that experiments at CERN's Large Hadron Collider had each observed a new particle in the "mass region around 126 GeV"[18] that was consistent with the Higgs boson predicted with the Standard Model. While it assists scientists in further work, the amazing discovery cannot account for the *why* of such a particle, or from Whom it came. Nor

---

[17] "What is the God Particle?" http://www.gotquestions.org/God-particle.html (accessed Feb. 11, 2016).

[18] CERN Accelerating Science, "The Higgs Boson," http://home.cern/topics/higgs-boson (accessed Feb. 11, 2016). The acronyms ATLAS and CMS represent two of seven major experiments in the Large Hadron Collider (LHC) project.

should one expect such explanations from these scientists because coming upon the "why" and "Whom" are outside the competence and expertise of those performing this amazing research. If the Higgs boson helps to support their scientific theory, the particle would already have existed within a universe created *ex nihilo.*

Scientists in their various disciplines are performing experiments that cause wonder. Sometimes a humorous incident provides a spark that ignites wonder at the interconnectedness of all creation. In late April, 2016, the Large Hadron Collider, called the world's most powerful scientific instrument, came to an abrupt halt. The 17-mile machine designed to smash protons at the near-speed of light simply stopped. Upon investigation, it was found that a small mammal – most likely a weasel – had gnawed through a power cable of the Collider.[19] Charred furry remains near the mishap revealed the problem. Speeding protons, small teeth, an electric cord, and a mammoth machine met, reminding a sophisticated society of John Muir's familiar observation: "When we try to pick out anything by itself, we find it hitched to everything else in the universe."

After astronauts had successfully landed on the surface of the moon and earthlings marveled at extensive data

---

[19] Geoff Brumfiel, "Weasel Apparently Shuts Down World's Most Powerful Particle Collider." npr.org, http://www.npr.org/sections/thetwo-way/2016/04/29/476154494/weasel-shuts-down-world-s-most-powerful-particle-collider (accessed May 1, 2016).

and moon-rocks gathered from earth's near-neighbor in space, astrophysicists knew an urgency to press for more extensive space travel allowing exploration of the galaxy we inhabit. After sending the exploratory "Rover" to Mars and initially studying what could be learned of that planet, there is an even more intense pursuit to determine what life forms may once have existed there and why they might have become extinct.

These are questions that invite fresh pondering because they affect, particularly in the present moment, still-deeper questions regarding the divine design of the universe, the meaning and preciousness of human life, and the relentless pursuit of technical innovation. Why is there the restless pursuit within science and technology to *direct and hasten evolution through human ingenuity*?

The urge to see farther into distant parts of the universe will only increase. As I write today, scientists are reporting a stunning discovery that will assist them in their search to understand gravity. An international team claims that after decades of trying, "They have observed the warping of space-time generated by the collision of two black holes more than a billion light years from Earth." They have detected "gravitational waves" that will "usher in a new era for astronomy..... It's the first time the Universe has spoken to us through gravitational waves.

Up until now, we've been deaf,"[20] said Professor David Reitze, director of the LGO project.

Colliding black holes, gravitational waves, and "a billion light years away from earth" – these are assertions about the larger universe that are mainly unimaginable for the human mind, yet they are part of the immensity within which humanity lives. Professor Karsten Danzmann from the Max Planck Institute for Gravitational Physics said, "It is the first ever direct detection of gravitational waves; it's the first ever direct detection of black holes and it is a confirmation of General Relativity because the property of these black holes agrees exactly with what Einstein predicted almost exactly 100 years ago."[21]

There is awe among the scientists who claim to have been addressed by "the Universe" in these "signals." Ghosh says that "Expected signals are extremely subtle, and disturb the machines, known as interferometers, by just fractions of the width of an atom..... On a graph, the data looks like a symmetrical, wiggly line that gradually increases in height and then suddenly fades away..... 'Gravitational waves go through everything. They are hardly affected by what they pass through, and that means that they are perfect messengers,' said Prof (sic) Bernard Schutz, from

---

[20] Pallab Ghosh, "Einstein's gravitational waves 'seen' from black holes," http://www.bbc.com/news/science-environment-35524440 (accessed Feb. 11, 2016).

[21] Ghosh, "Einstein's gravitational waves."

Cardiff University, UK."[22] While "black holes" have been the object of much attention, research, and probing of space for some time, Professor Gabriela Gonzalez says of the new discovery: "Now that we have the detectors to see these systems, now that we know binary black holes are out there – we'll begin listening to the Universe."[23]

Gifted scientists are willing to wait many years to hear possible signals that result from events occurring millions of light years away, "disturb" machines, and are recorded through symmetrical wiggly lines due to a collision of black holes! Yet, among those thrilled by this new discovery are persons who do not acknowledge the Creator who, *out of nothing*, fashioned this universe with incredible finesse and established an order so precise that millions of years later, humans could discover and marvel over actions and interchanges occurring in space – an outer space that seems so calm when viewed from earth on a serene evening, but in reality is constantly erupting with new wonders!

It is possible to live among profound mysteries and interchanges without adverting to the marvelous ways in which Providence is leading us. How heedful one must be to recognize the mysteries of every day, to listen eagerly, as professional scientists do, for even squiggly-line messages

---

[22] Ghosh, "Einstein's gravitational waves."

[23] Ghosh, "Einstein's gravitational waves."

from the "Universe" – in order to acknowledge and reverence the divine Designer.

Outer space is mainly a place of darkness in which uncountable galaxies move, with their billions of stars. It also teems with innumerable black holes and an immense amount of what is tentatively called "dark matter." So much of the universe remains "dark" to humanity and (at least presently) remains inaccessible to the most advanced telescopes. One of the greatest gifts in a restless creation is light, without which there would be no living creatures.

Light is radiant energy, the only form of energy that is visible. The wave-lengths of light that are visible to the human eye are only a small portion of the electro-magnetic spectrum – a spectrum that includes a series of rays having different wave-lengths. People of ancient times appreciated the preciousness of light in ways that we have lost because in many parts of the world, light is "on" unceasingly both night and day, available at the touch of a button. As a NASA description reminds us: without the sun, earth would be a ball of ice-coated rock. Without this source of radiant energy, no human, no living creature could survive. Although the sun appears to be a round and stable glowing disk, it is a mass of turbulent energy and outbursts spewing from it can "disturb" instruments and conditions on earth. Seemingly *still* and contained, it is perpetually in motion.

Both Testaments of the Bible speak with wonder of light and its meaning. The Gospel of John opens with a solemnity comparable to that of Genesis: "In the beginning was the Word, and the Word was with God, and the word was God. He was in the beginning with God; all things were made through him, and without him was not anything made that was made" (Jn.1:1-3) Then John writes: *"In him was life, and the life was the light of men. The light shines in the darkness, and the darkness has not overcome it."* (Jn 1:4-5)

Jesus identified Himself with light in one of the seven "I am" affirmations in John's Gospel: "I am the light of the world; he who follows me will not walk in darkness, but will have the light of life." (Jn 8:12) Jesus, Son of God, whose birth was made known to the Magi through the light of a star, personally identified Himself as The Light. In the natural universe that was made through Him, light is a radiant energy that sets in motion the multiple forms of living things. It is not surprising that at His Baptism the heavens opened above Him, nor is it surprising that Saul came to know Jesus' presence through light. The Acts of the Apostles says: "Now as he journeyed he approached Damascus, and suddenly a light from heaven flashed about him. And he fell to the ground and heard a voice saying to him, 'Saul, Saul, why do you persecute me?' And he said, 'Who are you, Lord?' And he said, 'I am Jesus, whom you are persecuting." (Acts 9:3-5)

God's answer to Saul reverberates with the experience of Moses in the desert of Midian when the divine presence was made known through fire and light in the burning bush. Exodus cryptically tells how Moses approached the bush which was aflame without being consumed. He was told to remove his shoes because he stood on holy ground. The One addressing him said "I am the God of your father, the God of Isaac and the God of Jacob." (Ex. 3:6) Upon receiving his mission to return to Pharaoh in Egypt and bring his people out of their oppression there, Moses asked God, if I come to the people of Israel with this message, and they ask your name, what shall I tell them? "God said to Moses, 'I AM WHO I AM.' And he said, 'Say this to the people of Israel, 'I AM has sent me to you.'" (Ex. 3:14) It was out of the flaming bush that Moses received this foundational revelation of the personal identity and reality of God as "I AM WHO AM," *personal, eternal existence* who promises to be with him. Light and fire are closely combined in divine revelation. After the people of Israel were freed from their slavery in Egypt and were journeying through the desert, an enduring "pillar of fire" by night, and a pillar of cloud by day enabled them to recognize that the divine presence was with them, guarding them: "And the Lord went before them by day in a pillar of cloud to lead them along the way, and by night in a pillar of fire to give them light, that they might travel by day and by night;

the pillar of cloud by day and the pillar of fire by night did not depart from before the people." (Ex.13:21-22)

Our having light accessible at all times – and the familiarity of the passage from Exodus regarding the pillars of fire and cloud can dull our sense of awe regarding both! Physicists tell of their tremendous excitement at detecting "subtle signals" that disturb their instruments only a "fraction of the width of an atom." Every swift lightning-rip through a dark cloud is a sharp reminder of a Burning Bush, a flaming pillar in the night.

We associate light and its unaccustomed absence with monumental events. When Judas and the crowd with swords and clubs arrived to arrest Jesus in the Garden of Gethsemane, there was darkness, and at his death on the cross, writes Luke, "It was now about the sixth hour, and there was darkness over the whole land until the ninth hour, while the sun's light failed, and the curtain of the temple was torn in two." (Lk. 23:44-45)

It was *at dawn*, the beginning of a new day, that Jesus' Resurrection was made manifest. Liturgically, in the darkness of Holy Saturday night, the celebration of the Resurrection begins with the lighting of the New Fire from which the Paschal Candle is lit. Its praises are sung as symbol of the Risen Lord. Near to tabernacles throughout the world, a burning sanctuary light signs Christ's abiding Presence. The second person of the Trinity is "light from light" and the Holy Spirit came on the morning of

Pentecost in tongues of fire accompanied by the rush of a mighty wind to manifest His presence.

There are several reasons why the rituals of light are especially fitting as signs of the divine presence and activity. There is a stirring immediacy about the speed of light, its presence and availability. How easily we say that the speed of light is 186,282 miles per second. Yet, *nothing* else in the physical universe exceeds this speed. To consider this more "visually," that means that light could circle the earth seven and a half times in one second. The energy of light travels in straight lines. Although it may appear to be white at times, light contains the whole spectrum of colors in all of their variety. Without light, there is no color. The visual splendors of creation are accessible to humans because the sun's rays shine on them and reflect onto their eyes.

Light shines equally on the good and the bad. Although it illumines vile activities, dung and decaying matter, it remains unsullied. Light illuminates and warms, but takes nothing away for itself – does not retain what it touches.

Dazzling discoveries of events that occurred billions of light years ago in outer space can make our present earth seem relatively quiet. From its inner depths to its outward "skin," however, earth is teeming with a necessary, inherent restlessness. Although we may not reflect upon it frequently, the physical earth is composed of three layers: a core, mantle, and crust. The compressed *inner* core of our planet is composed of iron, estimated to be about 10,000 degrees Fahrenheit (approximately the temperature of the surface of the sun). Already in elementary school, children learn that the outer part of planet earth's core is composed of extremely hot liquid metals about 1,400 miles thick. Outward from this core is a second layer of earth, the "mantle," composed of hot magma. It is also the location of huge tectonic plates of rock that sometimes shift, causing volcanoes and earthquakes to occur in the third and topmost layer, earth's crust.[24] It is on the uppermost surface of this crust that we have our dwelling place.

"All of Earth's layers, from core to crust, are in constant motion, caused by the flow of heat" says Tim Folger. "Researchers have known for many decades that the slow, convective sloshing of liquid iron in the outer core, aided by Earth's rotation, generates the planet's magnetic field."[25] The flowing molten iron creates electric currents which generate magnetic fields that bring about more electric currents and result in "a self-sustaining cycle called a geodynamo. Evidence from ancient rocks reveals that Earth's

---

[24] See "What is Earth's Core Made of?" http://wonderopolis.org/wonder/what-is-earths-core-made-of (accessed Jan.18, 2016).

[25] Tim Folger, "Journeys to the Center of the Earth," in *Discover Magazine*, http://discovermagazine.com/2014/julyaug/13-journeys-to-the-center-of-the (accessed Jan. 14, 2016).

geodynamo has been up and running for at least 3-5 billion years."[26]

How often do we think about, and thank our Father, who created all things through the Son, for what lies thousands of miles directly beneath our feet? As I write, our nation's flag is serenely rippling on the campus skyline. The regal pines that frame it give assurance that, at least temporarily, we can walk, work, build, and plant on the skin of earth's crust without being threatened by those molten fields of liquid metal roiling thousands of miles beneath our feet.

On cloudless nights, the sky reveals a related dark field of what seem to be fixed stars, but are actually masses of flame moving at high speeds. Above and below, the marvels of creation are always on the move. From one sunrise to the next, without flight plans or leaving home, we travel about 24,900 miles as passengers on earth's crust. No seatbelts are needed on this voyage, nor do we feel earth's daily spin. "It's because you and everything else – including Earth's oceans and atmosphere – are spinning along with the earth at the same constant speed."[27] *How often do we think about the fact that the Atlantic and Pacific oceans are moving with us, close to 25,000 miles each day?*

---

[26] Folger, "Journey to the Center of the Earth." Geophysicists continue to work at understanding *why* this can work as it does. See pp. 1-2.

[27] "Why can't we feel Earth's spin?" in earthsky.org, http://earthsky.org/earth/why-cant-we-feel-earths-spin (accessed Jan. 18, 2016).

At the same time, at an axial tilt, the spinning earth is orbiting around the sun at the rate of 67,062 miles per hour. We are moving through the cosmos simultaneously spinning and orbiting at dizzying speeds, yet unruffled robins land with curled claws on fragile twigs while sub-atomic particles race beneath the soil of Switzerland. We do not clutch the nearest railing to prevent slippage into outer space. As Sister Maura wrote:

Even a man who asks for miracles
would wonder
how to live with one
when it came to splitting the atom
of *known.*"[28]

There is more to ponder here. Even as scientists and technicians caution that the future is unpredictable, unknowable even in its possibilities, the "place" of our earth itself within the universe is changing. "You can't see it happening on Earth, but space itself is stretching. Ever since the Big Bang happened 13.8 billion years ago, the universe has been getting bigger. 'If you go into the distant future, everything that we see in the universe right now will expand away from us so much that we won't be able to see it anymore,' said David Schlegel of the Lawrence

---

[28] Sister Maura Eichner, "Not Entirely about Miracles," in *Walking on Water* (New York: Newman Press, 1972), 100.

Berkeley National Laboratory."[29] Since the measurements of time and space are immense, the expansion of the universe may seem unimportant for us, but as we reflect on current exponential change, it gives us pause to note "The universe grows every year, and by an increasingly larger amount."[30]

By comparing our daily, familiar experiences of movement and time to the gargantuan numbers, speeds, and distances just considered, we *seem* to make aspects of the moving universe more thinkable and more reassuring. Some have known what it is to live for a time in outer space and still fewer have walked on the surface of the moon.

A MOON-WALKER'S REFLECTIONS

Captain Bill Irwin, one of the astronauts who did walk on the moon, described what happened to him as a member of the Apollo 15 flight. He almost missed the opportunity. He knew great satisfaction in being a test pilot and was in the final year of age eligibility for the astronaut program when NASA received him into training for a moon-flight. In the Prologue of his book *To Rule*

---

[29] "The universe is expanding, but how quickly?" http://www.cnn.com/2014/04/08/tech/innovation/universe-expansion-astron. (accessed Jan.18, 2016).

[30] "The universe is expanding."

the Night, Irwin shared what it meant for him to make that journey, to look back at earth, first when it looked like the size of a basketball, then a golf ball, and finally a marble. Irwin said that it was only after his return from the journey that he was able to reflect on the reality that the Lord wanted him to go to the moon so that he could come back and do something more important with his life than fly airplanes.[31] He'd been absorbed in preparing for the journey and didn't know what the spiritual flight could be, he said, but during the flight there was a new sense of self, the earth, and God's nearness:

> We were outside of ordinary reality; I sensed the beginning of some sort of deep change taking place inside of me. Looking back at that spaceship we call earth, I was touched by a desire to convince man that he has a unique place to live, that he is a unique creature, and that he must learn to live with his neighbors.[32]

Irwin described an experience that he had while carrying out an activity away from the Lunar Module on the

---

[31] See James B. Irwin with William A. Emerson, Jr., *To Rule the Night: The Discovery Voyage of Astronaut Jim Irwin* (Nashville, Tennessee: Broadman Press, 1982), 17.

[32] Irwin, *To Rule the Earth*, 17-18.

moon's surface. A key string broke, and he couldn't set up the science station as planned. He said that there wasn't time to ask Houston because that would have involved a delay. He prayed and immediately had the answer. It wasn't just a vague direction, he said, but almost God telling him what to do, and he had a sense of divine presence. The privilege of being part of the moon journey was greater than his own, said Irwin:

> Indirectly, everyone on earth was a part of this flight. It was a human effort..... Everybody wants to talk to a man who's been to the moon. They think that since he has seen something they have not seen and will never see, he must know something they do not know..... They are interested in what happened inside us, in our hearts and souls. They can't go to the moon, but they can take this flight..... I can't imagine a holier place.[33]

In a later chapter, it will be possible to note how radically the moon missions have been superseded in plans of space travel far beyond earth's closest neighbor and how rapidly technical instruments are fashioned that

---

[33] Irwin, *To Rule the Earth,* 18, 22.

plunge ahead in exploring space, profoundly affecting the human future.

FROM THE ENORMOUS TO THE MINISCULE

Consider next the corresponding restlessness of the infinitesimally small aspects of creation. They, too, disclose how intensely creation has been "on the move" from the beginning. Peter Tyson reminds us of our intimate bodily involvement with the whole of universe: "Every single atom in your body – the calcium in your bones, the carbon in your genes, the iron in your blood, the gold in your filling – was created in a star billions of years ago. All except atoms of hydrogen and one or two of the lightest elements. They were formed even earlier, shortly after the Big Bang began 13.7 billion years ago."[34] While Tyson uses the inelegant label "Big Bang," he is speaking of "in the beginning," of that commencement of creation that set all in motion, and that continues to unfold in the mystery of our participation in what began billions of years ago. Tyson scientifically revels in affirming:

> The story begins at the beginning, as in the Big Bang. That is when, astrophysicists say,

---

[34] Peter Tyson, "The Star in You," in *NOVA: science NOW*. http://www. pbs.org/wgbh/nova/space/star-in-you.html (accessed Jan.19, 2016).

all the hydrogen in the universe came into being. Initially it was just protons, and then, as the young universe expanded and cooled, these became bound to electrons, forming hydrogen atoms. The very hydrogen atoms in the H2O that makes up over half your body were born then. They didn't come from your parents; they came from the early universe. Did you have any idea you have atoms in your body that are over 13 billion years old? ..... every other chemical element, including carbon, oxygen, nitrogen, and all the other elements essential for your life, is thought to have been fabricated in stars.[35]

Jesuit philosopher and paleontologist Pierre Teilhard de Chardin summarized the wonder of such realities when he said: "Hitherto, the prevailing view has been that the body....is a fragment of the universe, a piece completely detached from the rest and handed over to a spirit that informs it. In future, we shall say that the Body is the very Universality of things..... My matter is not a part of the universe that I possess totaliter: it is the totality of the Universe possessed by me partialiter."[36]

---

[35] Tyson, "The Star in You."

[36] Pierre Teilhard de Chardin, *Science and Christ* (New York: Harper and Row,1968),12-13.

It is only in recent centuries that scientific evidence has been able in an ever deeper fashion to verify many of the multiple ways that interchanges occur within the universe. When "transcribed" into the numbers and language of ordinary human experience, they help us touch the hem of the garment of human comprehension regarding the universe (many of these findings, even at their best, still remain open to further verification and/or correction). Persons of faith can move within an ever expanding awareness of the often startling mysteries of the created universe, able to praise and thank the Creator for the challenge and gift of living in the twenty-first century. Humanity has been prepared to keep moving out farther into the gifts of the universe, humbled not only by current wonders, but by the realization that all of this will ultimately give way to "a new heaven and a new earth."

Long before Pope Francis wrote his papal encyclical, *Laudato Si*, on human responsibility for care of the environment, St. Gregory of Nazianzen said in a sermon: "Let us put into practice the supreme and primary law of God..... To all earth's creatures he has given the broad earth, the springs, the rivers and the forests. He has given the air to the birds, and the waters to those who live in water. He has given abundantly to all the basic needs of life, not as a private possession, not restricted by law, not divided by boundaries, but as common to all, amply and in rich measure."[37] In *Laudato Si,* Pope Francis cites the concern of his papal predecessors for protection of the earth and the wanton abusive activities that contaminate, and threaten the existence of many earthly creatures:

> The violence present in our hearts, wounded by sin, is also reflected in the symptoms of sickness evident in the soil, in the water, in the air and in all forms of life. This is why the earth herself, burdened and laid waste, is among the most abandoned and maltreated of our poor; she 'groans in travail' (Rom. 8:22). We have forgotten that we ourselves are dust of the earth (cf. *Gen.* 27); our very bodies are made up of her elements, we breathe her air and we receive life and refreshment from her waters.[38]

---

[37] Saint Gregory Nazianzen, "*Oratio 14, De pauperum amore,*" 23-25, in PG 35, 887-890, as given in the Office of Readings for Monday of the first week of Lent, in *The Liturgy of the Hours,* Vol. II (New York: Catholic Book Publishing Co., 1976), 97.

[38] Pope Francis, Encyclical *Laudato Si: On Care for Our Common Home,* #2,1. http://w2.vatican.va/content/Francesco/en/encyclicals/documents/papa-france (accessed May 3, 2016).

ROOTS, EXTENSIONS, AND RELATIONSHIPS

A priest who understood this "violence present in our hearts" was Father Raymond Ellis, pastor of then-St. Cecelia's Parish in the inner city of Detroit, Michigan in the 1960's. When he was a young child, Raymond's family had emigrated from Lebanon to the United States. His parents did not speak English and seemingly those facilitating the entrance of foreigners at Ellis Island were unsure of his family's name. So, on entering the United States, the family name was listed as "Ellis." From the eastern coast of the United States the family moved to Detroit's inner city where Irish immigrants had settled. There, the olive-skinned boy from Lebanon learned to speak English with an Irish brogue. Some years later, Raymond was ordained a priest of the Detroit Diocese and before long was appointed pastor of St. Cecelia's Parish in the inner city.

Detroit's inner city, like so many others, was restless in the 1960's. African-Americans had replaced the earlier immigrants and were living in homes rented from landlords, many of whom did not provide proper upkeep and repairs. Neighborhoods were in disarray, people dispirited. Father Ellis described what he encountered when he came back to the locale where he had grown up. He found a sense of hopelessness among the inhabitants there. He saw that most of the windows in the parish school had been smashed over the summer and the alleys were splotched with over-flowing garbage containers. He began to share with members of his parish, and with others concerned about conditions there (Catholics were only 2% of the approximately 40,000 people living in the boundaries of St. Cecelia's) how they might revive hope and a realization of personal dignity. What he saw beneath desperate conditions was not only interracial struggle and the degradation of persons, but also that of the earth and all creation. To all who would listen, he began to speak of *roots, extensions and relationships.*

I spent a short time at St. Cecelia's when Father Ellis, collaborators, and members of the parish were trying to initiate an integral sacramental presence in their area. When invited to address a group of Catholic educators in Minnesota, Ellis described their efforts.[39] He said "Three years ago before we knew who we were as a people, we were the enemy, the cemetery dropped out of the sky. We were a 'nothing people' to the kids of the community – but last summer *one* window was broken in the school and that was accidental."

A basic premise of Father Ellis' convictions about "roots" was the meaning of choice. He explained that choice is never limited to one. God chooses all. In creating one man and one woman, God chose all. Abraham was chosen

---

[39] The author took personal notes from Father Raymond Ellis' presentation. Quotations cited in this chapter are from those notes, not from a published text.

by God, but in choosing Abraham, God promised that He chose also his many offspring. In choosing Abraham, said Ellis, God chose Christ. When He took the chosen people out of Egypt, He didn't reject all the others, but His acceptance of the Israelites was His sign of choosing all. To illustrate this, Ellis used a simple example. If I say that I like peanuts, he said, I don't have to *eat all peanuts.* It's how I take one from the bowl, how I eat it with relish that says I like peanuts – not just this peanut, but all peanuts. "All that I need to do to tell you that I like apples is to eat *one* with delight."

"*If I choose you, I've got to choose the whole universe,*" said Ellis. *"I choose everything if I choose you."* It may seem that in choosing one, all others are rejected, but the opposite is true. He referred to the work of Erich Fromm who said that for a man to love one woman – he must love not only all other women, but all of humanity. It is an aberration to reject all others when choosing one. The present crisis, said Ellis, is not a lack of love for everybody. Rather, the *crisis* concerns the inability to love one.

In showing the truth he was trying to convey, Ellis said that it helps to understand how God loves. When He put His arms around Jesus in the flesh, the Father was saying yes to all humanity. "He had to choose flesh," said Ellis, "because it has something to do with you and me." He chose *all* humanity. He had to choose all his roots, all his relationships. *In choosing to become one with this flesh, He had to choose sun, earth, moon, water, and people.* He was coming into relationship with *all. By embracing man He embraces the world of the spirit, all of flesh, all of the cosmos.*

Father Ellis explained that the first thing he had to do when he came into the inner city as pastor was to help people know who they are. What is man anyway? asked Ellis. It means first of all that it is necessary to have roots. These go deep, deep into the past.

No matter how far back you go, humanity is taken from humanity. Father Ellis spoke of his personal life when asserting that we all carry the scars of our past. A doctor explained to him why he had a thin white ring around the iris of his eyes. It was a kind of family trademark. Years ago, the doctor told him, there was starvation in your family and you are carrying the damage that was done 100-150 years ago. "The sperm cells in my body carry thousands of people, each who gave enrichment. There is a wealth of genetic continuity that has the ages for their parents," said Ellis.

Not only is a person's identity known in its roots, but also in its *extensions.* Father Ellis told educators how important it is to tell children "I live inside of you. I must, because you have your eyes open, and when your eyes are open, I am going right inside your mind. My image is flashing on your retina and your mind is making a conversion of that and you know me, and you know my image and you will recognize me." What we hear, touch, experience – is all filed away within us. The earth translates into eatable form what we eat. "I really become what dirt is," said Ellis. "I and the soil are in union. The sun bakes itself within me. When I take Vitamin C it's the sunshine in me. To understand the Incarnation, you have to understand what man is."

Relationship was Father Ellis' third emphasis. He told the parish janitor, "You touch me every time you mop a floor or wipe a wall. Mary Magdalene touched Jesus' skin, but you touch every student by the way you care for the school. We extend ourselves to the wall, sky and moon. It becomes part of our being. What Alan Shepard and his companions did, we did it, too. *We are a universe. We are one thing and we are relationships.*" Relationships are at the center of the matter because grace is relationship, love is, the Eucharist is, the sacraments are – and the Church is a body of relationships.

Ellis went on to explain in Eucharistic-understanding the meaning of relationship. Although he had left his parish to travel and give the presentation in Minnesota, he said "I have left my parish but my parish is within me. It's related to everything that's going on in my parish. I am here, but between me and them there is a bond, an invisible bond..... To touch me is to touch my whole parish. If something happens to me, that touches my parish."

Father Ellis lived what he taught. There were significant changes in that inner city neighborhood. He began to hire young men to clean the parish buildings and to plant grass and flowers. One of the first projects that he started was the proper disposal of garbage. Working side by side with the young men he hired, Ellis taught the truths of faith as he taught procedures. Looking at the contents of a garbage pail he would link them with the second chapter of St. Paul's Letter to the Philippians. The grapefruit rinds and coffee grounds in the garbage pails had been "poured out" for the benefit of those who had consumed them. How does one show respect for them? Give them a decent burial! That meant closing them securely in a bag and properly disposing of them.

Father Ellis was troubled that in a time of racial unrest, all the images and paintings of the parish Church portrayed Christ, Mary and holy personages as Caucasian. His prayer and concern led him to speak about this with a black artist, a member of the parish named Devon Cunningham. Ellis asked if Devon could paint a "Black Christ" in the dome of the sanctuary. He thought he could. When the scaffolding was erected, Devon had to test his own ability to work from it because he has a fear of heights. When completed, the powerful figure of the Black Christ caused a sensation in Detroit and beyond. It was pictured on the cover of both *Ebony* and *Life* magazines.

One evening Father Ellis went to see the film *Patton* in a local theater. When attendees filed out, a man remained seated. It was Father Ellis' body. Rosary in his hands, he had died of a heart attack. A photo taken after his funeral

Mass showed young black servers, crowded about the hearse that bore his body. They were weeping, knocking on the windows, and calling out "Don't leave us!" It was unscripted, living testimony of the reality of roots, extensions and relationships in a universe created to be at-one with the Creator. Ellis had a holy restlessness.

How does this relate to the meaning of holy "rest"? Christ invited his apostles returning from their mission to "Come away by yourselves to a lonely place, and rest a while." (Mk. 6:31). On another occasion He encouraged his followers: "Come to me, all who are heavy laden, and I will give you rest. Take my yoke upon you, and learn from me; for I am gentle and lowly in heart, and you will find rest for your souls. For my yoke is easy, and my burden is light." (Matt. 11:28-30). In a splendid article "On Restlessness," Antonio Lopez begins by saying that Scripture tells us that when God finished his creation he "rested to take delight in it (Gn 2:2-3; Ps 149). It also tells us that he commanded man to rest (Ex 16:29-30; 20:8-11), so that he might consider the greatness of the nuptial vocation to which he is called (Hos 2:18-20; Eph 5:32). This command contains, too, the promise that man may finally enter into God's own rest,"[40] finding peace and remaining in God's love.

How, then, is this to happen? In a universe created constantly in motion, in which human persons themselves

---

[40] Antonio Lopez, "On Restlessness," *Communio* 34 (Summer, 2007), 176.

participate, what does it mean "to rest," and to enter into God's own rest? Lopez points out that God also is ever present and engaged with human persons, always "at work" as John 5:17 says.[41] Rest does not mean the cessation of all movement. To "sleep in peace" is the still point that comes from "rightness" of relationship, which ultimately finds its perfection in the inner life of the Trinity.

---

[41] Lopez, "On Restlessness," 176.

Chapter II

"Seized By The Restlessness Of God"

Faith draws us into a state of being
seized by the restlessness of God, and it makes us pilgrims
who are on an inner journey towards the true King of
the world
and his promise of justice, truth and love.'[42]

*I*n the universe that throbs, spins, and expands
at increasing speed, there are multiple kinds of
restlessness and interactive forces. Eric Mataxas writes
that "the fine-tuning necessary for life to exist on a planet
is nothing compared with the fine-tuning required for
the universe to exist at all. For example, astrophysicists
now know that the values of the four fundamental forces

---

[42] Pope Benedict XVI, Homily for the Solemnity of Epiphany, 2013, cited in the editorial "Our Epiphany," *National Catholic Register*, Dec. 27, 2015, 12.

– gravity, the electromagnetic force, and the "strong" and "weak" magnetic forces – were determined less than one millionth of a second after the big bang. Alter any one value and the universe could not exist."[43]

If we knew *only* this much about the constant interplay of movements in our universe, it could astound us every day of our lives – but there is a tendency to take the most basic and astounding things for granted. As the poet Sister Maura Eichner wrote:

We walk in miracles as children scuff
through daisy fields.....
Common as spring, as bread, as sleep, as salt
the daisies grow. Our Father made them reel
against us like the morning stars that vault
the greater home His love will yet reveal.[44]

Blessed to be embodied human persons, we participate in the cosmic dance from the beginning of our existence. In the natural beginning of human life, a sperm

---

[43] Eric Metaxas, "Science Increasingly Make the Case for God," *Wall Street Journal*, Dec. 25, 2014, http://mail.google.com/mail/u/0/?tab=wm (accessed Jan. 23, 2016). Metaxas added: "For instance, if the ratio between the nuclear strong force and the electromagnetic force had been off by the tiniest fraction of the tiniest fraction – by even one part in 100,000,000,000,000,000 – then no stars could have formed at all. Feel free to gulp."

[44] Sister Maura Eichner, "We Walk in Miracles," in *Walking on Water: Prayer Poems* (New York: Newman Press, 1972), 20.

must go on journey to unite with an ovum. The Catholic Church teaches that when that union occurs, a "spiritual soul is created immediately by God – it is not produced by the parents – and also that it is immortal: it does not perish when it separates from the body at death, and it will be reunited with the body at the final Resurrection."[45] With the initial union of soul and body, as miniscule as the material component is, there begins a lifetime of "being on journey." From conception onward, a human person naturally conceived within the body of its mother must be restless not only to survive, but to participate in intense interchange with her. Like other newly-conceived children, the Incarnate Son of God entered human life in such smallness. Luke's Gospel tells of sixth-month old John the Baptist leaping within Elizabeth's womb when Mary came to her, bearing the so-recently conceived Jesus.

In the liturgical calendar of the Roman Catholic Church, the Feast of Epiphany is traditionally celebrated on January 6. The word "Epiphany" means "manifestation," and refers particularly to the revelation of Christ's divinity to the gentiles. The liturgical feast of the Solemnity of Epiphany, however, marks *three* revelatory events in the life of Jesus. First, he was visited by Magi who, Matthew's Gospel says, were "wise men from the East" who came to Jerusalem seeking him because "we have seen his

---

[45] *Catechism of the Catholic Church*, 2nd ed. Libreria Editrice Vaticana (Washington, DC: United States Catholic Conference, 1997), #366.

star in the East, and have come to worship him." (Matt. 2:2) Second, the Epiphany celebrates the Wedding Feast in Cana of Galilee, the village celebration of a marriage where Mary prepared the way for Jesus' extravagant miracle: changing water into wine. John's Gospel names it the first of Jesus' "signs" and that it "manifested his glory." (Jn 2:11) The third manifestation celebrated on Epiphany is Jesus' baptism by John the Baptist in the waters of the Jordan River. (see Matt. 3:13-17) When Jesus rose from the water of the Jordan, the heavens opened, the Holy Spirit descended upon him, and he was revealed as the beloved Son of the Father. Following his baptism, says the Gospel of Matthew, "Jesus was led up by the Spirit into the wilderness to be tempted by the devil." (Matt. 4:1) Each event presaged a vital "moving on."

Pope Benedict XVI's Homily for the Solemnity of Epiphany, 2013, vibrates with the significance of ongoing journeys and pilgrimages. It is faith, he said, that draws us into "*a state of being seized by the restlessness of God, and it makes us pilgrims who are on an inward journey towards the true King of the world, and his promise of justice, truth, and love.*"[46]

Even brief experiences of the interrelationships among humans on journey, wonders in nature, and awareness of divine presence give a personal sense of rightness

---

[46] Pope Benedict XVI, Homily for the Solemnity of the Epiphany, 2013.

from beauty-in-motion. Consider common examples. The film version of *The Music Man,* released in 1962, begins with a spirited rhythmical dialogue among salesmen aboard a passenger train that is slowing down as it enters "River City, Iowa." As the train slows in this classic work by Meredith Wilson, the phrases of the salesmen match the rhythmic clicking of the train car's wheels. There is more than charm in the rhythmic union of eyes and minds, screenplay and melody. There is a sense of "rightness" and delight in what is synchronous and "beautiful" in its unique genre.

Similarly, photographer of wild life, Dylan Winter, expressed his wonder and delight after he filmed the flights of "starlings" over an English heath at dusk. In his video, starlings flow across a winter evening sky, a half-million wings beating together. Without touching, the birds billow into the soft sky in swiftly changing cloud-shapes. In their rapid, restless flight they sky-dance at great speed as if all were parts of one body. It is restless beauty made visible and the flights of starling flocks are appropriately called *"murmurations."* In the psalms, the word "murmur" is used to name the soothing sound of the harp. Dylan Winter has combined instrumental melodies to his videos of murmurations. The rhythms of instruments and bird patterns blend well.[47] There is a purpose

---

[47] *"Dylan Winter and the Starling Murmurations,"* You Tube. See also another flight pattern in http://www.youtube.com/

in the starlings' coordinated movement over the heath. It prepares for their swift descent into a reedy habitat for the night, free of predators. Dylan notes how the birds fly "like a living organism." In the video, when he completed his filming, the photographer turned to leave, tripod on his shoulder. After an encounter with inexplicable loveliness, the man who has filmed wild life for thirty years said that he's thinking "How wonderful is that!"

The liturgy of the Easter Vigil brings about a unity of natural beauty, human bodily experience and a sense of divinely given "rightness" when the new fire leaps into the night sky, the Easter candle is blessed, and the "Exultet" is sung:

O truly blessed night
when things of heaven are wed to those of earth
and divine to the human.
Therefore, O Lord,
we pray you that this candle,
hallowed to the honor of your name,
may persevere undimmed,
to overcome the darkness of this night.
Receive it as a pleasing fragrance,
and let it mingle with the lights of heaven.
May this flame be found still burning

---

watch?v=eakKfY5attmY (accessed Jan. 30, 2016).

by the Morning Star:
the one Morning Star who never sets,
Christ your Son,
who, coming back from death's domain,
has shed his peaceful light on humanity,
and lives and reigns forever and ever.[48]

That the rhythmic wheels of train cars and the flowing flocks of starlings can speak to us so poignantly has to do with what Pope Benedict calls *"the restlessness of God."* As noted, he used that phrase in his homily for the Feast of Epiphany which honors the journey of the Magi, the Wedding Feast of Cana, and the Baptism of Our Lord. Each of these mysteries of faith incorporates unique aspects of the physical universe that move within them, and touch the deeper heart-call to relationship. The Magi discerned a star moving with purpose: the divine sign accorded with their field of expertise. Recognizing its significance, they were inspired to take up a divinely-prompted pilgrimage. In Cana, those who gathered to celebrate a marriage experienced a transformation of water into wine provided with largesse by *the* Bridegroom who would fulfill its deeper meaning in the Paschal Mysteries to come. At Jesus' Baptism, water from the Jordan flowed over the

---

[48]   *The Exsultet: The Proclamation of Easter,* usccb.org, http://www. usccb.org/prayer-and-worship/liturgical-year/easter/easter- (accessed May 4, 2016).

Son of the eternal Father, and He publicly began his salvific walk to Calvary.

In his first homily as Holy Father, Pope Francis said of the three readings proclaimed in that day's Mass: "I see that there is something in common: it is movement. In the first reading, movement is the journey [itself]; in the second reading, movement is in the up-building of the Church. In the third, in the Gospel, the movement is in [the act of] profession: walking, building, professing. Walking: the House of Jacob. 'O house of Jacob, Come, let us walk in the light of the Lord.' This is the first thing God said to Abraham: 'Walk in my presence and be blameless.' Walking: our life is a journey and when we stop there is something wrong."[49]

We know the devastation of "something wrong" when a loved person's heart becomes silent after a stroke, or when someone, having lost hope and meaning, severs the paths of blood flowing in and out of his heart. To say that there is passionate joy in the union among stars, flesh and a pilgrimage is not to deny the realities of pain and darkness that permeate even the finest of them. Long before the Passion of Jesus, the Magi committed themselves to make a journey that would accomplish their search, but initiate an even more difficult requirement – to return home in "a

---

[49] *"Pope Francis:1ˢᵗ homily, Missa pro Ecclesiae in the Sistine Chapel,"* Vatican Radio trans. http://www.news.va/en/news/pope-francis-1st-homily-full-text (accessed Jan.26, 2016).

different way." We are familiar with Christmas cards that portray three splendidly-attired kings holding their gifts gracefully in upraised arms as they ride clean-cut camels across placid sands. On these glowing greeting cards, even though three kings ride through a sunlit, cloudless landscape, the Star of Bethlehem gleams brightly in daylight before them. In his "Journey of the Magi," however, T. S. Eliot presents a different scene, writing as if he were one of the Magi, musing years later over the star-led trek:

> A cold coming we had of it,
>
> just the worst time of the year
>
> For a journey, and such a journey:
>
> The ways deep and the weather sharp,
>
> The very dead of winter.[50]

Eliot's king recalled how the camel-men cursed and grumbled, and ran away in their desire for liquor and women. "A hard time we had of it," he said. Villages were dirty, prices high, and voices sang in their ears "that this was all folly." The king also recalled, however, that there was a turning point. The royal travelers reached a temperate valley, and though the locals had no information about the child they sought, the three searchers continued:

---

[50] T. S. Eliot, "Journey of the Magi," *The Complete Poems and Plays*, 1909-1950 (New York: Harcourt, Brace and Company, 1952), 68.

And arrived at evening, not a moment too soon
Finding the place; it was (you may say) satisfactory.
All this was a long time ago, I remember,
And I would do it again, but set down
This set down
This: were we led all that way for
Birth or Death?[51]

There was certainly evidence of a birth, he said, but this was different. This was a hard, bitter agony for us, like death (our own death) as we returned to our Kingdoms. We weren't at ease anymore in the old dispensation where alien people clutched their gods. In fact, the old king said that he would be glad of "another death."

A Christmastide editorial in the *National Catholic Register* focused on the description of the Wise Men's journey found in Matthew's Gospel. The editorial writer noted how the courage of the men from the East still inspires our spiritual pilgrimage, and quoted an observation of Pope Francis in his homily for the Feast of the Epiphany in 2015. The Pope said of the Magi: "They passed from human calculations to the mystery. This was their conversion."[52] One moves differently toward mystery than toward what is perceived simply as a yet unsolved problem.

---

[51] Eliot, "Journey of the Magi," 69.

[52] See "Our Epiphany" in *National Catholic Register*, Dec. 27, 2015, 12.

OUR HEARTS ARE RESTLESS

Why does Saint Augustine's impassioned cry "Our hearts are restless until they rest in Thee!" have a perennial freshness after nearly seventeen hundred years? Enduring truths bear that kind of power. Augustine chose to affirm the individual person's restless journey through one of the most meaningful of human symbols, the heart. The physical heart is a concrete, bodily expression of what moves in the deepest interior of a person. The wonder of the physical heart itself defies ordinary explanation. (Could this even partially explain why many creative persons in past times attempted to invent "perpetual motion" in metal and wood?)

A New Health Guide affirms that an embryo's heart begins to form soon after fertilization – at barely two weeks of life. "By the fifth week of the gestation period, the heart starts beating and divides into chambers..... So you can hear a baby's heartbeat at six week gestation." [53] Jesus' Sacred Heart would have been beating vigorously by the time Mary returned to Nazareth from Elizabeth and Zechariah's home in the hill country. "How many beats do we get in a lifetime? If an individual averages 80 beats per minute, that's 4,000 beats per hour, 115, 200 beats per

---

[53] "When Does a Baby Have a Heartbeat?" newhealthguide.org, n.d. 1. http://www.newhealthguide.orgWhen-Does-A-Baby-Have-A-Heartbeat.html (accessed Jan. 26, 2016).

day, and more than 42 million per year, which calculates to roughly 3 billion if you live to age 72. When you think about them that way, heartbeats are the most precious commodity on the planet."[54]

The physical heart of Jesus remains one of the predominant signs of Christ, articulating his love and mercy. The word "heart" when used to express the interiority of the human person indicates *the deepest core of personal presence, love and intent.* It denotes the depths of the invisible soul that is often referred to as the inmost *spirit.* The "heart" is the interior reality of a person, fully known only to God, and only partially known by the self as the center of conscience, love, intention, emotion – and their true state of being in relation to God, other persons, and the created universe. "The Bible mentions the human heart almost 300 times. In essence, this is what it says: the heart is that spiritual part of us where our emotions and desires dwell ..... since God has emotions and desires, He, too, can be said to have a 'heart.' We have a heart because God does. David was a man 'after God's own heart.' (Acts 13:22)."[55]

---

[54] Dr B, "Just How Many Heartbeats Do We Get?" ushealthworks.com, http://www.ushealthworks.com/blog.index.php/2011/09/just-how-many-heartbeats-do-we-get/ (accessed Jan. 27, 2016).

[55] Got Quesions.org Home, "What is the heart?" http.//www.gotquestions.org/what-is-the-heart.html.(accessed Jan. 28, 2016).

Every person is called to wholeness, the inner "heart" to be at-one with what is expressed in and through the body:

> The human person, created in the image of God, is a being at once corporeal and spiritual..... it is because of its spiritual soul that the body made of matter becomes a living, human body; spirit and matter, in man, are not two natures united, but rather their union forms a single nature.[56]

To speak of a "restless heart" then, is to name an abiding restlessness of the entire person. "We come into this world with insatiable desires, huge talents, boundless energy, and grandiose dreams," says Ron Rolheiser. "Like a god or goddess, we'd like to drink up the planet, taste every wine, and know every experience; but, in all this desire and potential, we, all of us, eventually find ourselves in a very limited, circumscribed place and situation."[57] It all comes down, Rolheiser said, to this little space in history which, as good as it is, will fall short of our expectations. He recalls Henry David Thoreau's comment that although

---

[56] *Catechism of the Catholic Church*, #362, #365.

[57] Ronrolheiser.com, "Naming Our Restlessness" http://ronrolheiser. com/naming-our-restlessness/#.VpUqKXlliM8 (accessed Jan. 29, 2016).

we dreamed of building a bridge to the moon when we are young, by mid-life we pick up the materials and build a woodshed. Every person is called to a life-realization that involves a journey inward/outward. *Every day is a going where we have not been before.* It is not a question of distance. Jesus, Son of God in the flesh, experienced earthly human life within the parameters of space which we now call "Holy Land" – except, as Matthew says, for his infancy sojourn in Egypt (Matt. 2:13-15). Through Mary, his restless human ancestry flowed in his blood. He penetrated into the deepest realities of human hearts and relished time on the Sea of Galilee, and in nearby mountains. When misunderstanding and envy needed to be met with truth and set straight, He did so with elegant simplicity, informing questioners where He stood in divine identity of person: "Before Abraham was, I am." But he knew the ways of Abraham, the ways of a pilgrim.

The call and mission of Abraham, our "father in the faith," as narrated in Genesis, begins with a divine injunction to set out under divine direction: "Now the Lord said to Abram, 'Go from your country and your kindred and your father's house to the land I will show you.'" (Gn. 12:1) Abram was seventy-five years old when he set out from Haran with his wife Sarai, his nephew Lot, together with the "persons and possessions" they had acquired, and traveled to the land of Canaan, to Shechem, to the oak of Moreh. There, the Lord appeared to then-Abram and promised that he would give this land to his descendants. The patriarch went onward to Bethel and then to the Negeb. When a famine came there, he left for a sojourn in Egypt, he and his kin leading a nomadic life. Following divine guidance, he returned to Canaan where he pitched his tent, built an altar, and dwelt by the oaks of Mamre at Hebron.

Genesis then narrates compactly how Abram led his trained men in rescuing Lot from his captors, how he was met by Melchizedek, who brought bread and wine and blessed Abram. All of these things that Genesis relates had been directed by the Lord. How many criss-crossings, how many uprootings does it take before one is ready and there is a certain "fullness of time" for a breakthrough moment to occur? It was a long time for the old couple.

When Abram and Sarai were dwelling "by the oaks of Mamre" Genesis says that "the Lord" appeared to him "in the heat of the day" as he sat at the door of his tent." (Gn 18:1) When Abram looked up he saw three men approaching, whom he received with immediate reverence and lavish hospitality. God-surprises would follow that encounter. God "cut covenant" with Abram; a son was born to the aged couple, and their names were changed to Abraham and Sarah. In describing the couple's personal encounters with the "visitors" who came to their tent in the heat of the day, Genesis interchangeably speaks of the visitors as the *"three"* who came and *"the Lord."*

Becoming a wayfarer and then receiving wayfarers – these are particularly blessed events in the history of faith. The significance of our father of faith being a "wandering Armenian" is treasured in the collective memory of both Jews and gentiles. In her poem called "Abraham," the poet Jessica Powers speaks of him directly and warmly:

> I love Abraham, that old weather-beaten
> unwavering nomad; when God called to him
> no tender hand wedged time into his stay.
> His faith erupted him into a way
> far-off and strange. How many miles are there
> from Ur to Haran?.....
> I cry out: Abraham, old nomad you,
> are you my father? Come to me in pity.
> Mine is a far and lonely journey, too.[58]

When Sarah died, Abraham purchased a cave and its surrounding land in Hebron as a burial place for her. Later the cave also became his own burial place and that of Isaac, Jacob, Rebecca and Leah. Known today as the "Cave of Machpelah," it is the second holiest place (after the Temple Mount) for the Jewish people. The massive building over the burial ground was first erected by Herod in the Second Temple Period. When the people of Islam

---

[58] Jessica Powers, *The Selected Poetry of Jessica Powers* (Washington, DC: ICS Publications, 1999), no p.

conquered Hebron some seven centuries ago, they forbade Jews to enter the burial area, allowing them only to come as far as the seventh step on a staircase outside the building.

That barrier changed after the Six Day War in the 1960's. Israel regained entry to the sacred site, but unrest, violence, and military operations have since brought about changes in its inner appearance and accessibility. I remember visiting the memorial in 1969, shortly after the Six Day War and recall being very touched by the fitting way of communing with Abraham and his family there. Placed inside the main room of the memorial at the time was a fabric tent enclosed by protective roping. Canvas tent stools had been placed around it. It was explained to me that similar to the way that Catholics make offerings and light vigil candles at a shrine, one could make an offering and "rent" one of the camp stools for a time to honor the patriarchs and their wives, as a sign of their desire to remain present. How appropriate that the wandering nomad and his family would be remembered and honored in death as tent-dwellers, nomads on journey under the guidance of the Lord! Since that time of temporary tranquility in Hebron, intense clashes have occurred there, and the cloth tents have been replaced with other memorials within the building over the "cave," perhaps because the tents might provide hiding places for those bent on violence.

Over the millennium and a half years since Abraham lived, his descendants have repeatedly traversed the lands of the Near East. Famines and wars took them into Egypt – and then out of Egypt. The Chosen People, divided among themselves, came to know the destruction of the Temple and were taken into exile. Once more they were refugees in a foreign land, "hanging up their harps on tree branches," yearning for the days when they walked in the land of Promise, and freely made pilgrimages to Jerusalem and the Temple. At the decision of Cyrus, a remnant of Israel returned and rebuilt the temple. The heroes, heroines, and warriors of Abraham's descendants would be remembered for difficult treks and war campaigns: Deborah, Joseph, Moses, Joshua, Jacob, Rebecca, and Elijah among them.

It is the way of divine wisdom: to send out – and then in various ways, to accompany those sent on journey for specific missions. Joseph was sold to traders by his siblings, enabling him later to save his family in a time of famine. Unknowingly, by fleeing into the desert to escape retribution for killing of an Egyptian, Moses was being prepared for his destined mission to lead his people out of slavery. He could not have surmised that his escape from Egyptian wrath was only the beginning of another journey. It was on a stretch of desert, while tending the flocks of his father-in-law, that Moses encountered the presence of the living God at a burning bush. Having received his mission,

Moses became the leader of the Chosen people on their often-rebellious return to the Promised Land.

God did not send them on journey alone. Exodus also describes divine care for their food and water. Even more striking – God visibly, personally protected them. Long before the Magi would be given the guidance of a star, Exodus relates of the Israelites:"[T]he Lord went before them by day in a pillar of cloud to lead them along the way, and by night in a pillar of fire to give them light that they might travel by day and by night." (Ex 13:21).

When the long-anticipated Messiah came, from His conception in Mary's womb onward, He traveled on a path to His crucifixion outside Jerusalem. The author of John's Gospel was one of the hesitant young men who followed the finger of John the Baptist that pointed to Jesus as he walked along the Jordan River. When Jesus turned to ask what they sought, the young men wanted to know where he lived. "Come and see," Jesus said. Writing in his old age, John did not forget that encounter by the Jordan nor the times when Jesus would say "Come, follow me." We cannot estimate the number of miles that Jesus walked, even within the confined areas specified in the four Gospels. The evangelists repeatedly quote the Lord as saying "Come," "Go," and "Follow Me," "Take up your cross and follow Me," and "Launch out into the deep." He knew where His earthly journey would take Him and prepared His closest followers for readiness to be sent.

As He walked through Galilee, Judah, and Samaria, Jesus worked miracles and opened his followers to the unexpected potential in physical matter. From pilgrimages to Jerusalem for Jewish Feasts to trips to Caesarea Philippi for a time of rest and revelation – all led to his bone-grating walk up Calvary, carrying His cross.

At the Last Supper, before leaving the Upper Room for Gethsemane, Jesus spoke of His coming departure from them. While they could not follow Him immediately, He said, He was going to prepare a place for them so "that where I am you may be also. And you know the way where I am going." (Jn 14:3-4) When Thomas protested "Lord, we do not know where you are going; how can we know the way?" (Jn 14: 5) Jesus said to him: *"I am the way, and the truth, and the life; no one comes to the Father, but by me."* (Jn 14:6) He is at once the direction, the way, and the destination.

The activity of Jesus on earth continued after His Resurrection. He walked in the garden near His burial tomb to greet Mary Magdalen. In turn, He sent her on mission to the Apostles. He joined two of His disciples on the road to Emmaus, came back to the Upper Room, and at a later time prepared a lakeshore breakfast at dawn for Peter and his companions. Prior to His ascension, Jesus led the Apostles up the Mount of Olives from where He sent them on mission "into the whole world."

It is no wonder that the saints, mystics and poets write of the spiritual life as a *Way* to eternal life. St. Augustine sang from the depths of nuptial love: *"Fecisti nos ad te et inquietum est cor nostrum donec requiescat in te."*[59] This well-known acclamation is usually translated into English as "You have made us for yourself, O Lord, and our hearts are restless until they rest in you." The Latin word *te*, however, means "to" or "toward." More accurately understood then, the "way" is not a static state of being. Augustine's cry expresses a movement toward the beloved: "You have made us *toward* yourself, and our hearts are restless until they rest in you." In light of the entire theme of Augustine's self-revelatory writing in the *Confessions*, it is important to see this difference. The whole of creation bears the tremors, the resonances of love between Creator and all that is created, but salvation history tells over and over how human encounters with the Living God are calls *toward* ever-deeper union.

Saint Teresa of Avila and Saint John of the Cross did not have scientific information regarding the magnitude of galactic expansion, nor did they know of miniscule electrons moving among atoms beneath their feet as they journeyed over the coarse Castilian roads of Spain. What they *did* know was the mystical truth of restlessness: to be *"still and still moving / Into another intensity / For a further union,*

---

[59] Saint Augustine, *Confessions*, I, 1.

a deeper communion," of which T. S. Eliot wrote. Both Teresa and John wrote of pathways toward the Living Creator who, from nothing, set creation in motion with divine majesty and delightful whimsy. While both Teresa and John knew the call into ever deeper union with the Father, Son, and Holy Spirit as a restless journey, each described their love-search for spousal union with God through different images and metaphors of travel. Note how they differ and complement one another as male and female.

Saint Teresa of Avila, so recently named "Doctor of Prayer," described growth into union with God as an *inward* journey to the center of the person where the Master dwells. She could laugh at herself for trying to express ecstatic love of her divine spouse in the imagery of an "interior castle" where God dwelt at the center:

> Today while beseeching Our Lord to speak
> for me because I wasn't able to think of any-
> thing to say nor did I know how to begin
> to carry out this obedience, there came to
> my mind what I shall now speak about, that
> which will provide us with a basis to begin
> with. It is that we consider our soul to be
> like a castle made entirely out of a diamond
> or of very clear crystal, in which there are
> many rooms, just as in heaven there are
> many dwelling places..... and in the center

76

and middle is the main dwelling place
where the very secret exchanges between
God and the soul take place.[60]

There are seven major "dwelling places" (each having
myriad rooms) in Teresa's description of the Interior
Castle. There is need to advance from one inner dwelling
to the next. She warns against tarrying in a given dwelling
place and stopping the deeper movement toward union
with the Beloved.

Saint John of the Cross, who collaborated with Teresa
in the reform of Carmelite life in the sixteenth century,
describes the journey of the spiritual life in *outward* terms,
as an ascent up "Mount Carmel." John of the Cross was
artist as well as poet and mystic. He made sketches of "the
mount of perfection" for those seeking his spiritual direction. The sketches were small enough to fit into a book
of the Divine Office. In the sketches, the "path" of Mount
Carmel led straight to the top where an inscription read:
"Only the honor and glory of God dwells on this mount."
Branching off the straight path leading to the summit of
the mount were numerous material and spiritual pathways that could entice one from continuing the journey
to the summit. By these John placed an emphatic *"Nada"*

---

[60] Teresa of Avila, "The Interior Castle," # 1 and #3, *The Collected Works of St. Teresa of Avila*, trans. Otilio Rodriguez and Kieren Kavanaugh (Washington, DC: ICS Publications, 1980) 283-284.

to indicate "nothing" and the danger of departing from the journey to "plateau" on inadequate ways of trying to reach desired union with God. This demands renunciation which seems darkness, a "night" to the senses. In his introduction to *The Ascent of Mount Carmel,* Kieran Kavanaugh says "Individuals in their journey to God must go not by comprehending but *by not comprehending* and 'must exchange the mutable and comprehensible for the Immutable and Incomprehensible.'"[61]

T. S. Eliot's poem "East Coker" incorporates John of the Cross' imagery of the spiritual journey:

> Shall I say it again? In order to arrive there,
> To arrive where you are, to get from where you are not,
> You must go by a way wherein there is no ecstasy.
> In order to arrive at what you do not know
> You must go by a way which is the way of ignorance.
> In order to possess what you do not possess
> You must go by the way of dispossession.
> In order to arrive at what you are not
> You must go through the way in which you are not.
> And what you do not know is the only thing you know
> And what you own is what you do not own
> And where you are is where you are not.[62]

---

[61] *John of the Cross: Selected Writings,* edit and intro Kieran Kavanaugh, preface Ernest Larkin (New York: Paulist Press, 1987), 49.

[62] T. S. Eliot, "East Coker," 127.

I have often reflected with students on Eliot's relentless surety of the need to move beyond "where we are" and likened it to being at a kiosk in a large shopping mall. A kiosk presents a map of the shopping complex with a large black arrow pointing to a red dot and the message "You are here." No mall-attendee pulls up a chair and rejoices with a grateful sigh "Oh, I have arrived." Rather, the kiosk is simply a place-marker indicating possible destinations. One must choose and then decide the way to be followed. *"In order to arrive at what you are not / You must go through the way in which you are not..... And where you are is where you are not."*

Thomas Merton, Trappist monk, writer, and spiritual guide was a younger contemporary of Eliot. His writings and personal life vibrate with the unrest that erupted following World War II, the Holocaust, the horror of the atomic bombs dropped on Hiroshima and Nagasaki, and the search for relationship and shared insight with Eastern religions. Merton had converted to Catholicism at age 23 and entered Gethsemane Abbey in Kentucky just three years later in 1941. At his Abbot's direction, he wrote his early-life autobiography, published in 1948 as *The Seven Storey Mountain.*[63] His sudden death in Bangkok (accidental electrocution) brought anguish to his many followers.

---

[63] Thomas Merton, *Seven Storey Mountain* (San Diego, California: Harcourt Brace, 1948).

In a perceptive article, "Thomas Merton and the Eternal Search," published in the March 5, 2015 issue of *The New Yorker*, Paul Elie pointed to the concluding words of *Seven Storey Mountain*: "Here ends the book, but not the searching." Elie says that "Those words turned out to be as true as any Merton wrote before or after."[64] He described the book's concluding words as running against the spirit of the book which is "personal, casual, talky, and self-deprecating – the story of a conversion to Catholicism and a call to a Trappist monastery as the adventures of a young New York dangling man."[65] Elie says that Merton's fame, energy, and range of interests meant "that, in the postwar years, all Catholic roads ran through him," and that he described prayer "with the pure and uncut confidence that the object of prayer really exists and is not a product of the cultural imagination."[66] He was setting terms for readers of three generations, says Elie: postwar Catholics, 1960's "pilgrims" and "progressive contrarians."

Merton had a "tremendous dissatisfaction" for the world as he found it, says Elie. Even now, what's really striking is "just how deep his dissatisfaction ran and how high his expectations were for himself and for his life.....

---

[64] Paul Elie, "Thomas Merton and the Eternal Search," *The New Yorker*, Mar. 5, 2015, http://www.newyorker.com/books/page-turner/thomas-merton-and-the-eternal-search (accessed Feb. 3, 2016).

[65] Elie, "Thomas Merton and the Eternal Search," n.p.

[66] Elie, "Thomas Merton and the Eternal Search," n.p.

Here was a person who resolved not to miss the meaning of his life in the living of it. Here was a dangling man who was determined not to grow slack."[67]

In the Era of Restlessness and exponential change, circumstances and possibilities differ from the years of Eliot and Merton, but the *angst*, search, and need to effect what promises to fulfill the human heart only intensify. Many become distraught in their overt and often misplaced attempts to satisfy what really itches and scratches at the walls of their "interior castle," and what impedes the ascent of one's personal "Mount Carmel." Now that numerous possibilities of traversing the world are available, many in the human family are pushing from "where they are" to "where they are not." Increasingly, many who are persecuted and/or impoverished risk paying exorbitant amounts in order to risk passage to another place, often headed "where they know not" to escape from violence, slavery or death. There is, however, something still deeper that is occurring simultaneously, as described in the article "Risking death at sea to escape boredom," by Lucy Ash.[68]

The article shows that although many face great jeopardy in leaving their homeland, it is done in order

---

[67] Elie, "Thomas Merton and the Eternal Search," n.p.

[68] Lucy Ash, "Risking death at sea to escape boredom," BBC News, Annaba, Aug. 20, 2015, http://www.bbc.com/news/magazine-33986899 (accessed Feb. 3, 2016).

to survive. On the other hand, there are also many young Algerians who willingly risk death in crossing the Mediterranean because they are "fed up with lack of opportunities at home." Young men called "harragas" (Arabic for "path burners") try various ways of leaving Algeria permanently because they do not see a future with meaning in their homeland. Lucy Ash quotes a well-known Algerian writer, Kamel Daoud, who says that it isn't the economy that drives them to seek a way out. "They leave because here, in this country, their lives are pointless, there's no room to dream, and worst of all, there's no fun, no laughter, no kissing, and no colour."[69] Life in Algerian villages is described by Daoud as boredom that is "unrelenting, unbelievable, unbearable and inhuman."[70] The last statement, in light of the horrendous and death-dealing conditions for many of our brothers and sisters across the world, is another kind of cry from the heart. Young adults who find *boredom* "unbearable and inhuman" are on one of the "plateaus" which St. John of the Cross would describe as *"nada."* Who or what will awaken them from boredom to the deepest cry of their hearts and a call worthy of them? If not them, who will make "the deserts of Algeria" bloom in new ways for their people?

---

[69] Ash, "Risking death at sea to escape boredom," n.p.

[70] Ash, "Risking death at sea to escape boredom," n.p.

One thinks of young Augustine farther along the northern coast of Africa some seventeen centuries earlier, ruing in hindsight how he had sullied life and relationships there. Yet, despite immersing himself in all the sensual pleasures that he thought would satiate him, despite his brilliant successes in learning and rhetoric, despite his *freedom to leave his native land* and take up professional life in Italy, Augustine would fling himself down on the ground and groan "How long, O Lord, how long?" After his conversion, baptism, and finding the truths of authentic love that he had so desperately sought, Augustine could journey again *to* his homeland and pour out his life-energy in service there. The yearning and the journeys are not new, but the young men of Algiers will not know how and where to direct their intense desire for fulfillment until some "Monica" and/or "Ambrose" meets that intensity with truths and extravagant mercy worthy of their longing.

The world's peoples are on the move in numbers greater than have been seen before. Children and youths, women and men carrying bundles swarm eight-abreast across country roads, stumble through fields, and cross deserts to present themselves at the border of a nation that may or may not allow them to enter. As will be discussed in a further chapter, technical wonders and digital enhancements will not fill the heart's deep call for dignity, sustenance, relationship, and a purpose that exceeds the suffering endured. While political solutions are bandied about, the restlessness pressing up in the human family at this time is new in its demands and it will be new in searches for fulfillment.

Sometimes, setting out on journey is not a matter of necessity, or a means of escape from difficulties, but a choice that seeks fulfillment. The reality runs deep, catching up the physical and spiritual aspects of person into a bodily manifestation to go "where one has not been before." Pilgrimage is a theme of the spiritual journey to God. For more than a thousand years, for example, individuals and groups have chosen to set out on the *Camino de Santiago de Compostela* in Spain. Some set out directly from their homes to make the *Camino*, but from all over the world pilgrims come to walk, cycle, or ride on the "Way" to the Shrine of St. James in Compostela. There are many different routes to take, but the important thing is to make the pilgrimage.

"In an era in which it's easy to step on a plane and be deposited nearly anywhere in the world, the Way of St. James is a reminder of the power of pilgrimages taken slowly and deliberately. The path to Santiago de Compostela is meant to be walked, for the journey is as important as actually standing at the crypt of the apostle. Once all pilgrimages were made like this, journeys that took weeks or months of hard travel..... Its most important lesson is that a pilgrimage is as much about the journey as it is about arriving at the destination.[71]

There are pilgrimages which embody a summation of the different levels of restlessness described in this article, and which impel an increased restlessness. How could the Mother of God describe the enduring meaning of her visitation to Elizabeth? How could St. Paul simply re-tell what happened on the Road to Damascus – or the "two disciples" relate what happened when they walked with the Risen Lord on the night of Resurrection? Yet, all of them made known what *could* be said. It is a part of understanding the mystery and the gift of restlessness to recall life-changing "pilgrimages" in one's own life that have burrowed into the heart and impelled one to undertake the next journey.

As a child, I read Johanna Spyri's simple novel *Heidi*, that relates a young girl's adventures and life with her grandfather in the Swiss Alps. Reading it crystalized into a conviction that someday I would walk in those mountains and *know* and feel something that she knew. The Alps were etched on my soul-powers as a summation of what I yearned even as a child to climb and know bodily. Decades later, unexpectedly, I needed to go to Neuchatel for a few days in southern Switzerland. The low Jura Mountains

---

rise abruptly behind the city. On a Sunday afternoon I had a few hours of free time. I asked the locals if one could see the Alps from the crest of the Juras and received the suggestion: ride a nearby funicular up the steep mountain incline. Then, you will find out.

The funicular opened onto a spacious meadow where belled cows were grazing. No one was about, but far across the meadow was a gentle knoll. The only building in sight was a lone, steep-roofed chalet across the meadow. I thought: the dwellers in that home must know whether the Alps were visible from the knoll. When I knocked at the door of the chalet, a middle-aged woman answered, visibly surprised that a woman in a religious habit would come to her door. In halting English she said that the hazy sky might block any view of the Alps, but the knoll would be worth a try. I had gone for some distance and was startled when I heard someone running rapidly behind me. Turning, I saw that it was the woman from the chalet. Catching her breath she said that she and a friend were going to have the first cherry pie of the season made from cherries that her son had picked the day before. "Would I like to join them?"

We walked back to her home where a sturdy wooden table was set for dessert and coffee. The woman's friend was an elder whom I remember as an "image of Calvinism" in her chin-high black dress and swept-back hair. She spoke no English and I spoke no German. Brown rafters above our heads and the warmth of wooden furniture were the setting of charity that enclosed our holy meal. Simply, groping for adequate words, the three of us shared exquisite cherry pie and coffee, and the perfection of receiving and being received as "neighbors." It was a pre-Eucharistic meal, like a foretaste of what someday will enfold all honest differences in the Body and the Blood of Christ's embrace.

I could not have imagined that what was happening in that chalet was foreknown in divine wisdom when I yearned "for what I knew not" on Minnesota prairies so many years before, but still anticipated in the inner heart. I did not see the Alps that day – that would come later – but they were already within me. Cherry pie has never been the same since then. It is a sacred reminder. So far, what part of life's pilgrimage has touched your restless desires at unforgettable depths?

Pope Francis continues to underscore the importance of walking and continuing to walk together in faith. In his Angelus Address in Ecatepec, Mexico in February, 2016, he spoke to the people who had made the sacrificial journey to be with him, hear him, and pray for Mexico particularly. He said:

> How much each one of you has suffered to reach this moment, how much you have 'walked' to make this day a day of feasting, a

time of thanksgiving. How much others have walked, who have not arrived here and yet because of them we have been able to keep going. Today, at the invitation of Moses, as a people we want to remember, we want to be the people that keeps alive the memory of God who passes among his People, in their midst. We look upon our children knowing that they will inherit not only a land, a culture and a tradition, but also the living fruits of faith which recalls the certainty of God's passing through this land.[72]

Pope Francis emphasized the sacrifices of those who chose to walk to Ecatepec to join with him and their people for a celebration of the Mass and mutual support. Millions in the new millennium often choose or are forced to walk from homes – and homelands – not simply to overcome boredom but in order to escape brutal death or seek possibilities worthy of their humanity. A report from the United Nations High Commissioner for Refugees on June 18, 2015, made known the extent of a worldwide refugee crisis that has grown significantly within the past

---

[72] Pope Francis, "Angelus in Ecatepec: Let us give thanks," (En. radiovaticana.va, Feb. 14, 2016), http://en.radiovaticana. va/news/2016/02/14/angelus_in_ecatepec_let_us_give_ thanks/1208613 (accessed May 4, 2016).

few years. The report noted that "worldwide displacement was at the highest level ever recorded," and "the
number of people forcibly displaced at the end of 2014
had risen to a staggering 59.5 million compared to 51.2
million a year earlier and 37.5 million a decade ago."[73] The
report quoted Antonio Guterres, the UN Commissioner
for Refugees: "We are witnessing a paradigm change, an
unchecked slide into an era in which the scale of global
forced displacement as well as the response required is
now clearly dwarfing anything seen before."[74]

While all is in constant movement in the human heart,
certain times mark momentous turning points. The Age
of Restlessness names what is occurring at a scale never
experienced before. Crucifixions have returned in the
Asian Near-East; beheadings have once again reddened
the coast of the Mediterranean; evil is having its contemporary "hour." Yet, whatever the intensities of pain,
chaos and bewilderment, the "I AM" of the Burning Bush
is with us; the Risen Lord of the Eucharist is with us; the
Holy Spirit dwells within us. We are never alone on the
journey. A short portion of the well-known "St. Patrick's

---

[73] UNHCR, "Worldwide displacement hits all-time high as war and persecution increase," Global Trends 2014, News Stories, 18 June, 2015, http://www.unhcr.org/558193896.html (accessed May 5, 2016).

[74] UNHCR, "Worldwide displacement hits all-time high."

Breastplate" prayer is especially pertinent for this moment of pilgrimage:

> Christ be with me, Christ within me, Christ behind me, Christ before me, Christ beside me, Christ to win me, Christ to comfort me and restore me. Christ beneath me, Christ above me. Christ in quiet, Christ in danger, Christ in hearts of all that love me, Christ in mouth of friend or stranger.[75]

---

[75] Catholic Online, "St. Patrick's Breastplate," Prayers, http://www. catholic.org/prayer.php?p=550 (accessed May 5, 2016)

Chapter III

THE EUCHARIST, COMPLETE AND TRUE RESTLESSNESS

"*T*hus, the complete form of true restlessness, which is the true peace and rest, is Eucharistic, filial existence: man's life is taken up by Christ and brought into communion with the divine triune love; it is broken so that it can be continuously transfigured; and it is given away for the sake of others, so their lives, gathered in the *Christus totus*, may grow ever more in his beauty while resting in him who finds delight and seeks to rest in them.[76]"

Near the end of his book *Eucharist*, Robert Barron summarizes what happened to two disciples of Jesus on the evening of Easter. Downcast, they were walking home from Jerusalem and were joined on the road by the Risen Lord although they did not recognize Him. Barron

---

[76] Antonio Lopez, "On Restlessness," 200.

says "With delicious faux innocence"[77] Jesus asked what they were discussing as they walked. Cleopas relates (accurately, notes Barron) how Jesus had seemed to fulfill their expectations, but now he had been handed-over to the authorities and crucified. Some women were now claiming that He had risen. Jesus, in turn, asked the two disciples: wasn't it necessary that He suffer those things and so enter into His glory? Luke's Gospel says that Jesus, beginning with Moses, "interpreted to them in all the scriptures the things concerning himself." (Lk 24:27).

When the three arrived at Emmaus, Jesus gave the impression that He was going on farther, but the two invited him to stay. He did, and when they were at table, He "took the bread, and blessed, and broke it, and gave it to them. And their eyes were opened and they recognized him; and he vanished out of their sight." (Lk 24:30-31) Now they "got it," says Barron, and understood how all the events of Jesus' life fit together: "they *saw* Him," and in the next instant he disappeared. "Once they saw, they moved, this time in the right direction. Despite the lateness of the hour, despite the dangers of the road, despite the persecution that awaited them in the holy city, they got up immediately and raced to Jerusalem."[78] Note that a marvelous restlessness pervades the account of Emmaus. It began

---

[77] Robert Barron, *Eucharist* (Maryknoll, New York: Orbis Books, 2008), 138.

[78] Barron, *Eucharist*, 140.

as the disciples were walking "on the road," it continued in the intense conversation/revelation that climaxed in Christ's self-gift to them. Then, when He disappeared, the two disciples got up and raced to Jerusalem.

The Real Presence of Christ in the Eucharist can seem to be motionless. He is said to "repose" in tabernacles across the world. Christ's Presence in the Eucharist is the epitome of "still and still moving into another intensity for a further union, a deeper communion..." In his article "On Restlessness," Antonio Lopez offers an account of *how* "human existence reflects the presence of restlessness in rest. The call to incorporation into Christ is, in fact, an ever-restless, ever-resting growth within man of Christ – who comes to indwell with the Father and the Holy Spirit – and through the Holy Spirit, of man in Christ, the one sent by the Father."[79] Lopez' perceptive article moves from negative aspects of restlessness to "the positive sense of movement contained in 'restlessness.'"[80]

Before developing the positive meaning of restlessness, Lopez distinguished it from its negative and more obvious forms of *unrest*, which are so evident in current societies. He names several reasons for this unrest: the basic change that has occurred regarding the meaning of work; the "existential search for nothing other than sheer

---

[79] Lopez, "On Restlessness," 177.

[80] Lopez, "On Restlessness," 177.

novelty for novelty's sake"; the amassing of ever more material goods in order not to remember who is actually longed-for in each of these goods; and a saying "no" to that nuptial dialogue that God desires to have with humans. It is helpful to reflect on these insights before turning to the positive meaning of "true restlessness" in the Eucharist.

In exemplifying societal unrest in regard to work, Lopez says that work is now valued most for its income, and workers are tantalized by an onward and upward climb. This differs from former times when a parent or grandparent's accustomed occupation was often maintained for a lifetime. Many now consider this stultifying, an undesirable immobility. People are now willing to move from job to job, from one location to another as required to achieve their upward climb. They have to "keep going," says Lopez, so that in old age they might realize a sort of adolescence that is "blind to its mortality," spasmodic in its search for what is novel and exciting. There is an appalling "absence from oneself."[81] In vacancy from one's true self, there isn't a dwelling place where a person can be present *to oneself* and know authentic rest. Lopez cites Josef Pieper regarding the kind of restlessness that is dominant in the postmodern world: it not only "prevents the formation of culture and humane living, but, more importantly, originates in a human existence that is

---

[81] See Lopez, "On Restlessness," 178.

radically disengaged from itself and from history."[82] The anxious search to "move up" is often accompanied by an attempt to fill up with "things" what is actually lacking in the depths of the human being.

> In this second sense, as we mentioned, restlessness is an 'anxiety over' things because man continues to look, away from himself and from the real nature of what attracts him, for that Origin he does not really want to find. Restlessness, then, becomes the existential search for nothing other than sheer novelty for novelty's sake..... the anxious need to possess ever more new goods in order not to remember the one who is really longed for in each of those finite goods.[83]

In the United States, this is borne out in visible ways. Although many homes are larger now than those of fifty to one hundred years ago, there is not enough space in some of them to store the possessions acquired by their owners. It is only in relatively recent decades that even smaller towns and cities have row upon row of rental

---

[82] Josef Pieper, *Leisure, the Basis of Culture*, trans. Gerald Malsbary (South Bend, Ind.: St. Augustine's Press, 1998), quoted in Lopez, "On Restlessness," 178.

[83] Lopez, "On Restlessness," 179.

compartments to hold material goods that will no longer fit in homes or garages. Marketers use multiple forms of mass media to persuade potential customers that they *need* the most recent, most convenient, most technically competitive products to boost their social standing and supposed standard of living.

When Lopez speaks of adults who anticipate a late-life "adolescence," he touches a matter of great concern not only regarding work, but the meaning of aging. Elders have traditionally been esteemed as bearers of a heritage, as wisdom-persons who share with the young not only their personal memories, but the memories and valued experiences of those who have preceded them. The current content of many televised dramas and comedic programs reflects this change in understanding the meaning of elder life. Superficiality is evident in television-series that feature characters who are older buffoons rather than mature adults who have self-respect and appreciate a dedicated life seasoned by experience.

Two simple but concrete indicators of changed attitudes and practices concerning "growing old" are 1) the kind of greeting cards and gifts given for the celebration of birthdays and anniversaries; and 2) the burgeoning provision of artificial/technological elder-care including virtual pets and robotic attendants. Displays of greeting cards in retail stores have deteriorated in both the messages blatantly splashed across them and the crude images that accompany them. Numerous birthday cards contain tasteless messages that are typical of a pre-teen's awkward attempt at humor and feature gross references to body parts and functions in ways that denigrate persons of any age, but particularly elders.

Gift-giving to those advanced in years has also regressed. A few decades ago it would have been an insult to give an adult friend, spouse, parent, or grandparent a stuffed toy animal as a suitable gift. Now, however, advertisements abound for these products with visual support showing supposedly mature adults clutching, embracing and kissing huge teddy bears as if they were not only alive but a "someone" worthy of close relationship. The meaning of authentic *gift* has deteriorated in the United States. It will be important to return to this later in regard to Real Presence in Eucharistic life.

A second, but related, major shift is occurring in regard to personal bodily presence in caring for senior members of families, either in their homes or in institutions that provide services for elders no longer able to remain "at home." There is keen competition among companies that produce robotic toys and faux-person-machines designed to "care" for elderly persons who need assistance in practical matters of life such as eating, or simply rising from a bed or chair. Some robotic machines provide routine assistance. Of greater significance, though, is the designing of technical machines specifically intended to fulfill the human need for companionship. Japan, a leader in technology of this kind, is also having concerns about its aging population that increasingly lacks sufficient human care-givers. Since the future is bleak regarding the ratio of old and young, technical substitutes for a human presence are gaining popularity. In parts of the world where younger adults have become accustomed to technical replacements for real human presence, robotic substitutes for their elders already seems normal and desirable. A commentary on this trend reads:

> Wondering what to get an elderly relative this year? Just in time for the holidays, toy company Hasbro comes to the rescue with a gift for Grandma. The toy company is debuting a line of robotic cats the company says are 'designed to bring comfort, companionship and fun for your elder loved ones.'
>
> Named Joy for All, the new robot pet line is pitched as a way to keep the elderly company. The robotic cats come in three color patterns, have 'realistic' fur and make kitty noises and 'familiar cat-like actions'..... Billed as companion animals for seniors

rather than toys, Hasbro's site refers to the animatronic animals as 'companion pets.'[84]

In societies that lose respect for the genetic inheritance of children when/where they are conceived, and permit the "culling" and reformulation of newly-conceived fetuses before they are technically implanted in a woman's womb, there will also be diminished respect for an authentic handing-on of an individual's or a family's real history and genetic inheritance. This used to be the provenance of older relatives, but now they often have little sharing-contact with young children. It is a loss that corresponds to what Josef Piper points out as a loss of history in a culture.

The loss of personal intergenerational contact cannot be artificially replaced, and it affects not only human relationships, but receptivity for encounters with Divine Persons.

Lopez, in his study of restlessness – negative and positive – points to the clarification that came in Jesus Christ who urged anxious persons to relinquish a false understanding of God as a-personal, a being who is in immobile solitude. Rather, the Divine Trinity is a communion of love. Christ revealed a divine identity that made it possible to

---

overcome fearfulness of a pseudo-god that ultimately does not desire our good, that leaves the human person "orphaned," fending and planning ahead for self, and managing life on one's own. Such fear causes great unrest. It is the human "no" to the nuptial dialogue that God wanted to establish with man from the beginning. It makes a person feel orphaned and restlessly anxious about one's present life and eternal salvation, says Lopez. He cites St. Ambrose:

> I give thanks to our Lord God, who made a work of such a nature that He could find rest therein. He made the heavens. I do not read that he rested. He made the earth. I do not find that he rested. He made the sun, moon, and stars. I do not read that he found rest there. But I do read that He made man and then found rest in one whose sins he would remit.[85]

It is not human experience of *yearning* itself that brings disquiet, but the seeking of its fulfillment "in all the wrong places." There is a holy restlessness that differs from illusory forms of satisfaction that can never satiate the deepest longing of the human heart, and the actual

---

[85] St. Ambrose, *Hexameron*, VI 10, 76, trans. John J. Savage (Washington, D.C.: The Catholic University of America Press, 1961), cited in Lopez, "On Restlessness," footnote 21, 183.

call to union with the Trinity in Christ. Holy restlessness differs from anxiety, disquietude, perturbation and physical uneasiness. It can be very active as the *Song of Songs* exemplifies. The ardent expressions sing of love "strong as death.....its flashes are flashes of fire, a most vehement flame." (SS 8:6) We will return later in this, and the final chapter, regarding the "nuptial dialogue" that God desires to have with us.

In a culture that is experiencing a restlessness pervaded on the one hand by boredom, and on the other hand by anxiety, and frantic attempts to exceed all limitations, it is important to consider what constitutes a **blessed** restlessness that can coincide with an active peace and tranquility. Holy restlessness is closely allied with *real bodily presence, self-gift, abiding-in* another. In the Mystery of the Eucharist these reach their consummate realization within earthly existence. Preparation for encounters with the Real Presence of Christ in the Eucharist are developed through ordinary experiences of true body-presence, family meals and face-to-face conversation.

REAL PRESENCE

The Church names Jesus Christ's manner of presence with us in the Holy Eucharist a **Real Presence**. Each of those two words affirms a sacred truth of faith. In the mystery of Transubstantiation, a *real* and substantial change occurs. What has been unleavened wheaten bread, and wine processed from grapes, becomes *substantially* the living presence of the Body and Blood, soul and divinity of Jesus Christ. As long as the sacramental species remain, His abiding sacramental *presence* remains. Any precious blood remaining after the Eucharistic celebration is consumed, but the consecrated hosts kept in the tabernacle are reverenced as Christ's abiding Real Presence.

What does it mean to be *present* – or *absent*? "Being present" can have several levels of meaning. It can indicate that someone or something *exists* in a given place, or the *feeling* that someone or something is still "there" or remaining in a place. Presence can also mean a *quality* of person that makes others aware of them even when they are not overtly communicating or consciously trying to make their presence felt.

In recent decades, however, *connections* with others through electronic instruments (such as speaking on a smart-phone, texting, twittering, etc.) are also considered by some to be forms of "presence," and of equal worth or even preferable to face-to-face bodily presence. It is important to delineate the difference between real *bodily* presence and a more generalized understanding of what it means to be present – or what is touted as electronically "broadcast live." *Real Presence* participates in mystery – a reality so profound that it can never be penetrated completely. How presence is *understood* and the methods by which it is sought, radically affect human restlessness in the twenty-first century. They certainly influence an understanding of Christ's Real Presence in the Eucharist.

Relationships, both personal and communal, are interwoven with presence and absence. Arthur Vogel, writing of the meaning of bodily presence, emphasized that the human body *anchors* us in the world, "Personal presence is more than the body, but we are able to know it to be more only through the body and never without a body. Human presence needs the body in order to be itself, for body-meaning anchors us in the world."[86] He stressed that it is our *nature* to be body-meaning and a word. We really don't haves a choice about that. What we do have a choice about, said Vogel, is *"what we say with our body-words."* Words, wrote Vogel, are "meaning in matter, a location of presence, embodied presence. Meaning is in words as we are in our bodies, and it is only because we are bodies that we can 'be' our words – or as it is usually put, mean what we say."[87]

It is crucial to ponder the meaning of presence in regard to human restlessness because presence is actualized in our primary relationships with the Persons of the Trinity and our day-to-day relationships with other human persons. In the sixth chapter of John's Gospel, a

---

[86] Arthur Vogel, *Body Theology: God's Presence in Man's World* (New York: Harper and Row, 1973), 91.

[87] Vogel, *Body Theology*, 92.

moment of truth came to those who had followed Jesus into a remote place to be with Him, to receive his healing and teaching. They listened to Him, and were fed through His miraculous multiplication of loaves and fishes. Although they pursued Jesus around the Sea of Galilee to receive what He could continue to give them, they were closed to the kind of Real Presence he desired to be for them. They murmured, "Is not this Jesus, the son of Joseph, whose father and mother we know? How does he now say, 'I have come down from heaven'?"

Jesus spoke of a real presence that many could not accept. "I am the living bread which came down from heaven; if any one eats of this bread, he will live forever; and the bread which I shall give for the life of the world is my flesh..... For my flesh is food indeed, and my blood is drink indeed. He who eats my flesh and drinks my blood abides in me, and I in him." (Jn 6:51, 55)

Many of his followers left Jesus at that point because they could not accept this intensely intimate reality of real presence – His promise to be present and enter them as food and drink. How little the Apostles internalized this understanding at first! What Jesus promised was a depth of presence obviously unfamiliar to those who followed Him and heard Him speak. He did not use esoteric terminology, but rather opened a door for glimpsing ways of presence that only divine desire for union with human creatures could provide. Not only would Jesus be *present to* them, feeding them. He would enter them as a real presence of food and drink. The *Catechism of the Catholic Church* dwells on this:

> The mode of Christ's presence under the Eucharistic species is unique......In the most blessed sacrament of the Eucharist 'the body and blood, together with the soul and divinity, of our Lord Jesus Christ and therefore, *the whole Christ is truly, really, and substantially* contained.'[88] 'This presence is called 'real' – by which is not intended to exclude the other types of presence as if they could not be 'real' too, but because it is present in the fullest sense: that is to say, it is *substantial* presence by which Christ, God and man, makes himself wholly and entirely present.'

This marvelous, but spare, statement of the *Catechism of the Catholic Church* regarding the Real Presence of Christ in the Eucharist states a mystery beyond total human comprehension. Its truth could only be known through Christ's revelation. A genuine *revelation* is not something that can be discovered, or found through study and experiment. It can only be made known through personal choice. Divine

---

[88] Council of Trent (1551): DS 1651, followed by a quotation on real presence from *Sacrosanctum Concilium*, 7, in the *Catechism of the Catholic Church*, #1374.

revelation was made known through *divine* choice, not only for the good or consolation of those who received it, but for the benefit of all humanity. Divine revelation also brought a mission to those who initially received it. They were to make known what had been revealed and entrusted to them. This caused reverent fear, but the promise of divine assistance came with it. The prophets, Moses, Mary, the Mother of God, and St. Paul all came to know this. Revelation is:

> God's communication of himself, by which he makes known the mystery of his divine plan, a gift of self-communication which is realized by deeds and words over time, and most fully by sending us his own divine Son, Jesus Christ.[89]

The Apostles received the incarnate Lord bodily at the Last Supper. The Resurrection of Jesus and the coming of the Holy Spirit would enable them to realize at least partially what had been given to them and the mission that they now bore. The unfolding of all the implications and connections involved in this gift would continue, as Jesus promised when he said "When the Spirit of truth comes, he will guide you into all the truth; for he will not speak on his own authority, but whatever he hears he will speak,

---

[89] Glossary in *Catechism*, 897.

and he will declare to you the things that are to come."
(Jn 16:13)

While the marvels of restlessness in the universe, mysterious as they are, do not touch the depths of the Eucharistic mystery, pondering them can expand reverence for the *Eucharistic* mystery. The internal activities within an atom can be partially described, and the collisions of remote black holes delicately detected by instrumentation – but even then, their origin and response to laws not of human making cannot be explained scientifically. What multiple scientific discoveries *can* do is increase thankful wonder, and increase restless desire to respond ever more deeply to the revelation of Christ's Eucharistic self-gift. The truth of Eucharistic real presence had to be revealed, and no experimentation by the finest scientific instruments can tell of the "how and why" Divine Love chose this manner of a union beyond human love's devising.

Further, the presence of Christ in the Eucharist is the living *Risen Christ* whose Body and Blood are no longer subject to the perceptible characteristics of His presence in Galilee when He was a child, a carpenter, or a resident of Capernaum. Theologians vary in their theories and interpretations concerning Christ's risen body and His appearances prior to the Ascension. Some scholars think that Christ's risen body is a *physical* body capable of being seen normally in a space-time world, possibly even able to be photographed. Others affirm a bodily resurrection of Jesus but do not speak of it as a "physical" body. Scripture scholar Raymond E. Brown wrote of "a corporeal resurrection in which the risen body is transformed to the eschatological sphere, no longer bound by space and time – a body that no longer has all the natural or physical characteristics that marked its temporal existence."[90] The disciples from Emmaus, the Apostle Thomas, and the men who ate broiled fish with the Risen Christ on a lakeshore would have groped for words to explain how they experienced His risen body. What matters: it *is* the *Risen* Christ who is personally present Body and Blood, soul and divinity in the Eucharist.

At the Last Supper, Jesus told His apostles that it would be to their advantage if he left them "for if I do not go away, the Counselor will not come to you; but if I go, I will send him to you." (Jn 16:7) In Chapter 14 of his Gospel, John wrote that Jesus spoke directly of His desire that the Holy Spirit be their Counselor "to be with you forever, even the Spirit of truth.....you know him for he dwells with you and will be in you."(Jn 14:16, 17) The Holy Spirit would not simply come to visit them or provide occasional guidance. The promise was that the Holy Spirit would *dwell within* them. The real presence of Jesus' Body and Blood in the Eucharist and the real indwelling presence of the Holy

---

[90] See Joseph Smith, "N. T. Wright's Understanding of the Nature of Jesus' Risen Body," *The Heythrop Journal*, LVII, 2016, 30.

Spirit are foundational to divine ways of presence and holy restlessness.

Today, the desirability of real *bodily presence* to one another, among ordinary humans, is currently questioned and often avoided in favor of contact through technological media. It is with good reason that Antonio Lopez refers above to human "origins" and the "beginning" when discussing restlessness in present culture. What is the meaning of our bodily presence in the world? How does the divine intent "in the beginning" apply to real bodily presence now? When Pope John Paul II began his series of public Audiences on a Theology of Body and God's original design for human persons, he looked to the "beginning" as expressed in Genesis – even as Jesus did when he was questioned about the indissolubility of marriage (Matt 19:3-8). The revealed *divine intent* in creating a universe that culminated in humanity provides a key to the meaning of real presence. Man and woman were created in the divine image and likeness, and as a later chapter will discuss, there is no greater mutual presence than that among the divine Persons.

REAL PRESENCE AND ABSENCE

The counterpart of presence is absence. Until recently, there was a common (at least in a superficial sense) understanding of the difference between them. Now, however, what it means to be present or absent is contested in numerous ways. The "explosion" of technical instruments has brought about a reinterpretation of presence. The call "Beam me up, Scotty," associated with science fiction and the *Star Wars* series, suggested to the popular imagination a few decades ago that a person functioning in a sci-fi milieu could be transported in a de-materialized state and re-materialized again. It serves as an apt early example of a desired re-fashioning of the human body that would obviate the limitations of human bodily presence. N. Katherine Hayles wrote already in 1999:

> From my experience with the virtual reality simulations at the Human Interface Technology Laboratory and elsewhere, I can attest to the disorienting, exhilarating effect of the feeling that subjectivity is dispersed throughout the cybernetic circuit. In these systems, the user learns kinesthetically and proprioceptively, that the relevant boundaries for interaction are defined less by the skin than by the feedback loops connecting body and simulation in a technobio-integrated circuit.
>
> Questions about presence and absence do not yield much leverage in this situation,

for the avatar both is and is not present, just as the user both is and is not inside the screen.[91]

In his course on Theology of the Body at John Paul II Institute in Washington, DC, Monsignor Lorenzo Albacete pointed out that philosophy enables us to see the human body as the **language** of the human self, but theology of the body enables recognition of a greater clarity: "[T]he body possesses a **language** which enables it to proclaim and make present the life of God – more precisely, the Trinitarian Life of God."[92] That underscores the tremendous dignity of every human body-person (whether they are now living, or have lived, or will live).

The embodied person exists between two horizons. The two accounts of creation given in Genesis 1-2 constitute one horizon. In cryptic narration they present the beginnings of the cosmos and the creation of the first humans in relation to the divine Creator. The corresponding horizon is the future culmination of earthly human existence and the entire universe as we know them, and the coming of "a new heaven and a new earth."

---

[91] N. Katherine Hayles, *How We Became Posthuman: Virtual Bodies in Cybernetics, Literature, and Informatics* (Chicago: The University of Chicago Press, 1999), 27.

[92] Lorenzo Albacete, in Notes for Course on "John Paul II 624: Sacramentality of the Body," John Paul II Institute on Marriage and Family, Washington DC, 1.

(Rev 21:1) The boundary between them of which Genesis speaks is described as "the tree of the knowledge of good and evil." That tree is a symbolic expression of the covenant with God, broken in man's heart. It delineates two opposed situations: that of original innocence (that of a theological prehistory) and that of original sin, or historical human history. Pope John Paul II said:

> The state of sin is part of 'historical man,' of the human beings about whom we read when we read in Matthew 19, that is, of Christ's interlocutors then, as well as of every other potential or actual interlocutor at all times of history and thus, of course, also of man today. Yet in every man without exception, this state – the 'historical' state – plunges its roots deeply into his theological 'prehistory,' which is the state of original innocence..... *Thus, historical man is rooted, so to speak, in his revealed theological prehistory*; and for this reason, every point of his historical sinfulness must be explained (both in the case of the soul and of the body) with reference to original innocence.[93]

---

[93] Pope John Paul II, "General Audience of September 26, 1979," *Man and Woman He Created Them: A Theology of the Body*, trans and

While it is not possible to detail here the creation narratives' dynamic exposition of the creation of the universe and humanity *from nothing,* there is reverence and poetic beauty in Psalm 33's expression of the original divine design, in what the psalmist would call "the plans of his heart":

By his word the heavens were made,

by the breath of his mouth all the stars.

He collects the waves of the ocean;

He stores up the depths of the sea.

He frustrates the designs of the nations,

he defeats the plans of the peoples.

His own designs shall stand forever,

the plans of his heart from age to age.[94]

Centuries before the Incarnation, God was recognized by the psalmist as present, active: His own design would stand forever. Prior to the fall, in the state of original innocence, the man and the woman are described as peacefully, even delightedly present bodily. The Creator gave them the capacity to multiply, fill the earth and make it and all

---

intro Michael Waldstein (New York: Pauline Books and Media, 2006), 142-143.

[94] Psalm 33, *Liturgy of the Hours,* Vol. III, trans International Commission on English (New York: Catholic Book Publishing Corp., 1975), 731.

its inhabitants flourish. Created with free will, the parents of all future human beings were then *capable* of love and fruitful decision-making, but also capable of saying "no" to the divine design. The choice described as being made at the "tree" made it the symbolic boundary between a vibrant life in union with God, each other and the rest of creation – and a life wounded with multiple forms of dis-ease and unholy restlessness. These are so evident in "historical man" – in us, the women and men who live on this side of original sin, identified with Adam and Eve's choices made at "the tree."

A kind of hubris or bravado often characterizes the way in which humans look back to "the beginning" and to all that is summed up in the "Tree of good and evil." The meaning of real presence and absence changed. Genesis tells of the results of the Fall: Adam and Eve knew shame, tried to hide from God, and then began to excuse their guilt by concocting the "blame game." There was no expression of remorse, no asking for forgiveness. Hiding rather than transparent real presence became a characteristic of sinful humanity. Thus began the *unholy restlessness* resulting from rejection of relationship with God.

When trying to cope with the results of lost innocence, humans often turn to either flippancy and brash humor, or the proud assumption of a seemingly godly stance. Perhaps no other object/situation is so frequently parodied in humor as the Fall of Adam and Eve at the Tree in the Garden of Eden.

Each of the four Walt Disney World theme parks has an iconic image. Although few may consciously relate it to the Tree of Genesis, a "Tree of Life" is intended to epitomize and be an iconic image of Disney's Animal Kingdom Park. Consider the ironies of the name and the composition of the contemporary image. Called the "Tree of Life," the huge structure is only one of a few *artificial* "trees" among more than four million *living* plants in the park. Over 145 feet tall, its base is fifty feet wide. Made to resemble a bonsai tree, it has over 8,000 various-sized branches and more than 102,000 "man-made leaves" (each one foot long) that can blow in the wind. In the roots, trunk and branches of the structure are over 300 carved animal shapes, and inside the base of the tree is a small theater that repeatedly presents a 3-D film called "A Bug's Life." While it is a cleverly devised icon for the Animal Kingdom Park, it is a reminder that when the first humans rejected the original Tree of Life, they certainly did not know how much would be lost in its iconic translation! "Humankind cannot bear very much reality" T. S. Eliot wrote in "Burnt Norton."

> But as Eliot reminds us, authenticity isn't easy. Rather it is the most difficult thing of all. Acknowledging the reality of who

we are is the sort of enterprise that will inevitably fail unless aided by grace. The moment we claim to 'know ourselves' is precisely the moment when we are most prone to self-deception, especially if that knowledge is not mediated to us by the Word of God. Our age is one of deep confusion about the nature and authority of reality, and one of endless amusements to help us avoid it..... No generation has been able to bear reality – ours is simply the first that has been able to construct a virtual alternative that is more to our liking.[95]

Flannery O'Connor, a convert to Catholicism, through the characters in her short stories, wrote with stinging accuracy of the human search for fulfillment. Knowing that lupus was shortening her own life, she not only wrote incisively, but also spoke candidly of what mattered. In one of her letters to a friend she said that the Eucharist was the center of existence for her. Everything else in life was expendable. An often-repeated outburst of Flannery's occurred during a literary cocktail party.

---

[95] Matthew Lee Anderson, "Humankind Cannot Bear Very Much Reality," mereorthodoxy.com, http://mereorthodoxy.com/humankind-cannot-bear-very-much-reality/ (accessed Feb.16, 2016).

When conversation included a comment on the Eucharist as being a quite-suitable symbol, Flannery said of the Eucharist that if it *is* only a symbol "to hell with it." This incident occurred at the beginning of her writing career and she risked rejection on the part of seasoned writers for stating her faith so graphically.[96] What she knew was that everything depends on the reality of the Real Presence – as it did for those who received the teaching of its truth from Jesus Himself in Galilee.

> The Jews then disputed among themselves, saying 'How can this man give us his flesh to eat?' So Jesus said to them, 'Truly, truly, I say to you, unless you eat the flesh of the Son of man and drink his blood, you have no life in you..... For my flesh is food indeed, and my blood is drink indeed. He who eats my flesh and drinks my blood abides in me and I in him'..... This he said in the synagogue, as he taught at Capernaum. Many of his disciples, when they heard it, said, 'This is a hard saying: who can listen to it?' (Jn 6:52-53; 55-56; 59-60)

---

[96] See Barron, *Eucharist*, 95-96.

One has to have a certain respect for those who turned away and left Jesus when He spoke of the reality of His Body and Blood to be given to them as food. Not believing, they did not try to relativize what He said in order to have more free food. Did some of them return eventually?

A few years later, St. Paul was forthright in dealing with members of the early Church in Corinth. Responding to reports that there were abuses when they came together for the Lord's Supper, he explained its reality succinctly and then wrote: "Whoever, therefore, eats the bread or drinks the cup of the Lord in an unworthy manner will be guilty of profaning the body and blood of the Lord. Let a man examine himself, and so eat of the bread and drink of the cup. For anyone who eats and drinks without discerning the body eats and drinks judgment upon himself." (I Cor 11:27-29)

It is evident that personal evil sometimes recognizes the sacred Presence of Jesus in the Blessed Sacrament with greater acuity than believers who receive Him sacramentally. Luke's Gospel tells of Jesus' confrontation of evil spirits in the synagogue of His hometown of Capernaum: "And in the synagogue there was a man who had the spirit of an unclean demon; and he cried out with a loud voice, 'Ah! What have you to do with us, Jesus of Nazareth? Have you come to destroy us? I know who you are, the Holy One of God.' But Jesus rebuked him, saying 'Be silent, and come out of him!'" (Lk 4:34-35) Those who now are associated with satanic worship, or seek to produce "Black Masses," recognize the Real Presence and seek to obtain consecrated hosts in order to show hatred for Christ by performing obscene and vilifying acts with them. Out of love for the Real Presence, and to make reparation for offenses against the Eucharist, some parishes and faith communities are making chapels available for extended times of adoration of the Blessed Sacrament.

Once the reality of a body-to-body presence is recognized and lived with integrity, other ways of presence take on their own significance. This is also true in regard to Eucharistic encounters. A blogger identified as "Marc" writes perceptively of the contrast between presence and absence. He claims that "absence" would be just that: nothingness, the lack, the not-being-there of a particular person. The absence of a loved one though, "isn't that at all," he says. He describes feeling the absence of a *beloved* as an atmosphere of their unseen presence: "not so much gone as everywhere, the whole world crowded as a Parisian metro with their nearness."[97] He uses striking analogies. It is, he says, as if the hole spoke of its doughnut or silence sounded like the missing lover's voice. In short, he says, the physical relationship is possible only because of a person's existence, "the existence of a secret, inte-

97 Marc, "Presence as Absence," patheos.com, http://www.patheos. com/blogs/badcatholic/2013/12/presence-as-absence.html (accessed May 6, 2016).

rior spiritual life which expresses itself through the physical," adding:

> Christians, is this not how we relate to God
> and to the Saints? Is there any absence
> more present? Are we not flung hard
> against His person by the fact that He is not
> available to our immediate modes of relation? 'Because you have seen me, you have
> believed; blessed are those who have not
> seen and yet have believed.' (John 20:29)[98]

"REMEMBER ME"

Real bodily presence in daily life illuminates unseen real presence. In the celebration of the Eucharist, there is the love-directive of Christ: "Remember Me." In an unpublished, autobiographical article on his priesthood, physicist Father Robert Brungs reflected on his boyhood in Cincinnati, Ohio, during the great "Depression" of the 1930's. He recounted one of his clearest memories. He had come home from school on a gray, chilly November afternoon, and after he had hungrily consumed a "catsup sandwich," his mother told him to get his shoes and those of his sister from the shoe repair shop. His mother gave him

---

[98] Marc, "Presence and Absence."

a five dollar bill which he shoved into his pocket. Arriving at the store, he reached into his pants pocket for the money. "Instead of the well-worn bill, my fingers closed on nothing." It *had* to be there, he said! The shoe man was sympathetic "but in 1937 he wasn't going to forego his two or three dollars." Robert searched through soggy leaves on his way home and "with his heart in his mouth" he confessed the loss to his mother. She reached for her purse and took out the only thing in it – a ten dollar bill. She impressed him with the fact that the money had to last the family for the next four days. Hanging on to the bill as if his life depended on it, he retrieved the shoes and retraced his steps, kicking the leaves:

> About two blocks from the shoemaker's I found a soggy green five dollar bill lying on the sidewalk in plain sight. I couldn't believe it. It had not been in that spot on my terrible trip home or I certainly would have seen it. It could not have been lying out in the open for very long because it was a busy street and somebody would have found it ahead of me. And they would have kept it.[99]

---

[99] The selection from Father Robert Brungs, SJ, is from an unpublished essay, Sept. 25, 2002, intended for a work entitled *The Body Beautiful....to bring Christ to creation and creation to Christ*. The essay was edited and published posthumously by Sister Marianne Postiglione, RSM, in a memorial book honoring Father Brungs

The shoe repair man got his payment and Robert returned home. "Then with all the great subtlety a six year old boy can manage, I produced the ten dollar bill. But there was no fanfare." With the same equanimity she had shown at news of the loss, his mother told him "I suppose you'll be more careful with money in the future." Brungs wrote: "I have."

The reason for recounting this personal memory of Father Brungs is twofold. Like the memories written in the Gospels, incidents vividly recalled, and written down many years after they occurred, speak truths about real body and real presence in ways that differ from (but complement) carefully worded documents. Both are needed. What struck Father Brungs as he recalled the incident of the lost "fiver," was how clearly it remained in memory. "The fact that I can remember this event of 65 years ago with startling clarity – I can even see in my mind's eye individual red, yellow and brown leaves that I kicked – is proof to me of the significant part that afternoon played in the making of one man."[100] It wasn't just the money and the horror at its loss that made it so significant. It was relationship. Authors of the Gospels remembered (long after they occurred) specific details of daily life with Jesus

---

entitled *Written in OUR Flesh: Eyes Toward Jerusalem* (St. Louis, Mo.: ITEST Faith and Science Press, 2008), 7-8.

[100] Brungs, essay, Sept. 5, 2002.

that helped them become Eucharistic men capable of undergoing martyrdom.

Like Father Brungs' recollection of the color of leaves on a Cincinnati sidewalk, the evangelist John would remember the precise hour of the day that Jesus turned to him on a path along the Jordan; the number of barley loaves a boy had in a basket; and the exact number of fish hauled up on the shore before having breakfast with the Risen Lord. Experiences of *real presence* remain embedded in a person and can prepare one for deepened understanding of Real Presence in the Eucharist.

There is a second reason for recounting Brungs' seemingly minor incident: it shows reverence for bodied realities in the simplest of things. Jesus did not choose goblets from Herod's collection for the Last Supper, nor exotic foods from Egypt to be the means of the first transubstantiation. He chose what ordinary people knew: unleavened bread and the wine of a Paschal Supper. The restlessness that humans know in longing for *more* is often experienced close by, but ignored, or excitedly scrambled over in order to grasp what is sensational.

My religious community, the Franciscan Sisters of the Eucharist, has named extensions of the Eucharist into daily life "a field of presence." There is an enduring way in which Eucharistic presence extends beyond the celebration of daily Mass, the reception of the precious Body and Blood in Communion, and the sacramental presence of the Living Lord in the tabernacles of our Community Centers. There is an unseen aura that emanates from the chapels of the Community – not an imaginary "something," but a form of presence that is akin to "blogger Marc's" description of the seeming absence of one who is beloved: an "atmosphere of unseen presence" or "the whole world crowded with their nearness."

Having received the Risen Spouse in the Eucharist, each Sister can walk into her place of daily service – or suffering, or travel – conscious that the Blessed Sacrament she has received will, in union with the Holy Spirit and the Father, pervade the environment through which she passes. She becomes a kind of living monstrance through whom others encounter Christ. The desire within the Body of the Community is that the "field of presence" from Holy Communion will bring Christ's blessing to every situation. Whoever receives Christ in Holy Communion worthily has this incredible privilege. It is the mystery of St. Francis, so often cited: one day he invited one of the brothers to go into Assisi with him to preach. They walked through the city without saying a word to anyone. Upon their return, his companion asked why they hadn't preached. Francis replied "We did." No one can imagine what blessings extend from Christ when the Blessed Sacrament is carried in procession through the streets of a city or a university campus, or from the body-person of one who has received the Eucharist. There is a loving restlessness in the Real Presence.

RESTLESS BODY AND THE EUCHARISTIC MYSTERY

It is unusual that a surgeon would write about his practice in analogy to the Eucharist. Dr. Richard Selzer was an exception in that regard. He was a Professor of Surgery at Yale University and also became well-known as a gifted author during the last fifteen years before his retirement. In an essay entitled "Surgeon as Priest," he wrote of what it meant for him to enter the body of another in surgical care, and invited his reader to stand by him (as it were) as he did so. "One enters the body in surgery, as in love, as though one were an exile returning at last to his hearth, daring unchartered darkness in order to reach home."[101]

> Turn sideways, if you will, and slip with me into the cleft I have made..... Here, give me your hand. Lower between the beefy cliffs..... All at once, gleaming, the membrane parts....and you are *in*.

> It is the stillest place that ever was. As though suddenly you are struck deaf. Why,

---

[101] Richard Selzer, "The Surgeon as Priest," *Mortal Lessons: Notes on the Art of Surgery* (Simon and Schuster, 1977), 198.

when the blood sluices fierce as Niagara,
when the brain teems with electricity, and
the numberless cells exchange their goods
in ceaseless commerce – why is it so quiet?
Has some priest in charge of these rites
uttered the command 'Silence'? This is no
silence of the vacant stratosphere, but the
awful quiet of ruins, of rainbows, full of
expectation and holy dread. Soon you shall
know surgery as a Mass served with Body
and Blood, wherein disease is assailed as
though it were sin.[102]

Selzer knew an intimacy with body and blood, the
"stillest place that ever was" but a place teeming with
activity comparable to Niagara's fierce sluicing. He was a
doctor with the insight of a poet, who understood what it
means to be "still and still moving."

Both Father Robert Brungs, Jesuit physicist, and Dr.
Richard Selzer, surgeon, were *present* to what they experienced. Their keen remembrances had penetrated the body
of each, with immeasurable interconnections – memories
not only concerning personal relationships, but relating
to the earth and the larger creation. Father Robert Brungs
contracted polio when he was 2-3 years old, although his

---

[102] Selzer, "The Surgeon as Priest," 198.

parents did not realize it at the time. He spoke of his body as a-symmetrical in its growth. In later life, the effects of the disease of his childhood returned, bringing nagging pain, the required use of a cane, and the need to be seated when he celebrated Mass.

Each of the senses receives experience in its proper capacities. The sense of smell is the strongest in this regard. Some years ago, I taught a summer course at a woman's college, and invited students to know personally the strength of the sense of smell. I brought a small vial of perfume to class and invited the women to touch it to their wrists. The perfume had been prepared by a women's contemplative Community so that retreatants and visitors could obtain it at their Gift Shop and have a remembrance of their faith experiences there. The essence combined 14 fragrances from the Abbey's land, ranging from roses to alfalfa. After class, one of the women went to study at the college library. She was irritated by the actions of a young man who at first sat at her library table, and then followed her at a polite distance when she went to find a book in the nearby library stack. He finally said that he was exasperated. Shortly before this, he had made a retreat at a Trappist Monastery and it was "driving him crazy" that he was smelling the air of the Monastery when he was close to her. She explained the fragrance and both were relieved to know the connections among the contemplative centers, their land and fragrances. How potent is the use of incense in the Liturgy! Memories of sacred events are evoked when (even after many years) incense resembling the mixture used at a prior liturgical celebration is again offered in prayer. The body-person remembers, and activities proper to each of the senses can awaken and stir multiple interconnections.

MEAL

Blessed are children whose families regularly sit down to share a family meal together, where members "take in one another" as they take in the gift of food. In his thoughtful commentaries on *The Humanity of Man*, Edmond Barbotin probed the meaning of a meal. "The meal," he says, "is in fact the social activity beyond all others." It requires gathering in one place at the same time, and around one table. "It involves dialogue, a face-to-face encounter, and finally a specific communal action which gives all the factors just named their fullest meaning: the sharing of food."[103] Barbotin sees the table as the prime piece of furniture. Made for reunions, and intended to be surrounded, it invites and waits even when the rest of the room is empty. Of all foods shared there, bread (especially in countries where it is the basic food) can concentrate in itself the entire meaning of food. "The number of opera-

---

[103] Edmond Barbotin, *The Humanity of Man* (Maryknoll, New York: Orbis Books, 1975), 319.

tions required to produce bread makes it the symbol of human solidarity in work and in the will to live."[104] As will be discussed in the following chapter, the digitized milieu in which we live increasingly inhibits personal embodied experiences and relationships. This negatively intensifies already restive relationships, as seen especially in the way that food and meals are taken in haste, or isolation.

Sherry Turkle says in the opening pages of her book *Reclaiming Conversation: The Power of Talk in the Digital Age*:

> We have embarked upon a voyage of forgetting. It has several stations. *At first, we speak through machines* and forget how essential face-to-face conversation is to our relationships, our creativity, and our capacity for empathy. *At a second, we take a further step and speak not just through machines but to machines.* This is a turning point. When we consider conversations with machines about our most human predicaments, we face a moment of reckoning that can bring us to the end of our

---

[104] Barbotin, *The Humanity of Man*, 322-323.

forgetting. It is an opportunity to reaffirm
what makes us most human.[105]

Not only have we embarked on a "voyage of forgetting."
The very idea of what it means to have a meal "together"
is being lost for many. This inhibits an understanding
of Eucharist at a very basic level and needs to be faced
with new concern. In the first chapter of her book, Turkle
says "These days, we want to be with each other but also
elsewhere, connected to wherever else we want to be,
because what we value most is control over where we put
our attention."[106] She exemplifies this by sharing what it
means for "Cameron," a college junior in New Hampshire.
He told Turkle that he hates it when everybody puts
their phones next to them when they eat, and are always
checking them. When you're at dinner, he said, there is a
"rule of three as a strategy" to allow for continual scanning.
This means that when you are at dinner with a group you
have to make sure that at least three of them have their
heads up from their phones before you let yourself look
down at your own:

> Let's say we are seven at dinner. We all have
> our phones. You have to make sure that at

---

[105] Sherry Turkle, *Reclaiming Conversation: The Power of Talk in a Digital Age* (New York: Penguin Press, 2015), 16-17.

[106] Turkle, *Reclaiming Conversation*, 19.

least two people are not on their phones
or looking down to check something –
like a movie time on Google or going on
Facebook..... So I know to keep, like, two or
three in the mix so that other people can text
or whatever. It's my way of being polite.[107]

Turkle's observations will be seen in a larger context
in the following chapter. But in reflecting on Eucharist
and restlessness, it is important to hear what Turkle's
research shows about digital distance, control, and the
present move from conversation to "mere connection."
There can be a low level of body-to-body presence to one
another that misses the basic principle of humanity: created in the image and likeness of God, we are given life
for a communion of persons in and through the body. As
cited earlier, Anglican Bishop Arthur Vogel stressed that
we *are* "body-words." That isn't something we can change.
It is what we *say* with our body-words that matters.

Although Christ spoke bodily in all of his relationships,
the language of his own body-person at the Last Supper
was spoken to the utmost. In his Gospel, Luke writes
"when the hour came, he sat at table, and the apostles
with him. And he said to them, 'I have earnestly desired
to eat this Passover with you before I suffer'.....And he took

---

[107] Turkle, *Reclaiming Conversation,* 20.

bread, and when he had given thanks, he broke it and gave it to them saying, 'This is my body which is given for you. Do this in remembrance of me.' And likewise the cup after supper, saying 'This cup which is poured out for you is the new covenant in my blood.'" (Lk 22:14-15;19-20)

Christ tells His own that he has "earnestly desired" to eat this Passover with them. This is the apex of holy restlessness. Luke records that the Apostles were mainly obtuse to what Jesus was revealing and giving to them. A few verses later in this account of the Last Supper, Luke says that they began to argue among themselves who was the greater. Their superficial response indicates how little they understood at that moment that a divine person had given Himself totally in and through His body and Blood.

GIFT

If, as Turkle points out, there is a loss of difference between presence and absence today, a loss of the meaning of *bodily* presence and a shared meal, there has also been a loss in understanding and *knowing* the meaning of gift. How casually, in the bluster of searching for and purchasing gifts, the very depth of what they signify is lost. Yet, self-gift remains at the core of love, human and divine. The Gospels speak of the first Eucharist at the Last Supper as Self-gift. "This is my body which is given for you..... This cup which is poured out for you is the new covenant in my blood." (Lk 22:19-20)

What is an authentic gift other than a way of speaking bodily: this is myself given to you, for you? Prod your memory for the best gift you ever received as a child, as an adolescent, as an adult. What made them "best"? What made them memorable? The earliest childhood memory I have occurred when I was 2-3 years old and it involved a tiny gift. We were poor. My Dad had a part-time at the post office and when he delivered mail in cold weather, he wore an army-surplus overcoat and government-issued cap with a visor. My earliest memory? I went to the door of our home with my Mother to greet Dad when he came home from work one day. I still see him, tall against a golden-lit background. When we opened the door he told me "Find it!" That meant that I could search through his pockets one by one until I found a small wrapped piece of licorice candy.

The memory remains because it had all the qualities of a real gift. It was given out of thoughtful love. It was not something required, requested, ordered ahead of time. It was a totally unexpected surprise. More, it was person-to-person and appropriate. It meant that he had taken thought and sacrificed time to get the small delight and deliver it. Those are the *qualities* of a genuine gift, no matter how large or small the gift, no matter the age or gender of the recipient.

Consider how God gives gifts. Watch for the person-to-person elements of love, surprise, appropriateness, sacrifice, and thoughtfulness. Consider for example, gifts received by Our Lady, St. Joseph, Zacchaeus, Mary Magdalene, Martha and Mary, Nathaniel, Peter, and the Woman at the Well. The specific persons and occasions change radically, but the elements of true gift remain. Jesus continues to speak bodily in the Eucharist: this is I, Myself, given for you.

In earlier chapters there has been discussion about restlessness in the physical universe and the human person on journey as pilgrim. These reflections apply to the Eucharist and the real presence of Christ in his self-gift. If particles from a star are in interchange with our body persons and all we touch, what does that tell us about the holy restlessness of the seeming stillness of the Eucharistic Presence?

In the moment of Incarnation, the Son of God began human life in its smallest physical form, invisible to the unaided human eye: the epitome of smallness, help-lessness and vulnerability. There is an active restlessness in the Eucharist that accords with the moment of Incarnation. God changes substantially the tiny host and a small amount of wine into Christ's Presence. The Second Person of the Trinity becomes dependent in an extraordinary way – the sacramental host has to be taken up, physically handled, and given through humans who may be weary or careless. One of the greatest aspects of the Eucharist is that the Lord of the Universe becomes totally vulnerable, and completely given in a form absolutely necessary for human existence: consumed as food and drink. Those who have suffered helplessness in their confinement, dependency, and the threat of abandonment and death, know a companion in the Savior of humanity. Vietnamese Cardinal Francois-Xavier Van Thuan lived this communion with the Risen Lord in his imprisonment, without trial, for a period of thirteen years, nine of these spent in isolation.

> During this time, his hope was buoyed through the Eucharistic celebration, through which he transformed his cells into veritable chapels. Using breadcrumbs and wine, smuggled in under the guise of stomach medicine, he consecrated the bread and wine in the palm of his hand into the Body and Blood of Christ.[108]

The millions of persons who are exiled, persecuted, terrorized, enslaved, or confined in hospitals and in all

---

[108] catholicnewsagency.com, "Long-jailed Vietnamese cardinal set on path to sainthood," Oct. 23, 2010, http://www.catholicnewsagency.com/news/long-jailed-vietnamese-cardinal-s (accessed May 6, 2016).

forms of helplessness share a closeness to the Lord of the Eucharist, who, in loving restlessness, desires to feed them with His Body and Blood.

Chapter IV

RESTIVENESS IN A
CYBERNETIC ENVIRONMENT

cyberspace: Definition: Imaginary, intangible, virtual-reality realm where (in general) computer-communications and simulations and (in particular) internet activity takes place. The electronic equivalent of human psyche (the 'mindspace' where thinking and dreaming occur) cyberspace is the domain where objects are neither physical nor representations of the physical world, but are made up entirely of data manipulation and information. Canadian science-fiction writer William Gibson (1948 -) who coined the term....describes it in his 1984 novel 'Neuromancer' as 'consensual hallucination'....graphic-representation of data abstracted from every computer... unthinkable complexity.'[109]

The Third Millennium has commenced with a technically-induced restiveness among persons of all ages. Fifty years ago, most people across the world would not have heard of "cyberspace," nor grasped its description as an "imaginary, intangible, virtual-reality realm" of "unthinkable complexity." Now, many of the world's inhabitants are steeped in that realm and take it for granted as inescapable.

Coping with the instruments of communication, for example, can be overwhelming. Consider the swift proliferation of paraphernalia associated with Smartphones and the Internet, and the constant prodding to upgrade them, or replace them with more advanced models. For more than thirty years, Sherry Turkle, Abby Rockefeller Mauze Professor of the Social Studies of Science and Technology at MIT has studied the impact of contemporary technology on the human person. In particular, she has focused on the effects that technology has on children and young adults who have grown up from infancy with electronic instruments in their hands and pockets.

---

[109] businessdictionary,"What is cyberspace? definition and meaning," http://www.businessdictionary.com/definition/cyberspace.html. (accessed Feb. 20, 2016).

Turkle, a licensed clinical psychologist, is recognized as an expert in perceiving what is happening to individuals and the world community under the influence of these instruments. In her book *Alone Together: Why We Expect More From Technology and Less From Each Other*, Turkle writes:

> But this is not a book about robots. Rather, it is about how we are changed as technology offers us substitutes for connecting with each other face-to-face..... As we instant-message, e-mail, text, and Twitter, technology redraws the boundaries between intimacy and solitude..... Teenagers avoid making phone calls, fearful that they 'reveal too much.' They would rather text than talk. Adults, too, choose keyboards over the human voice. It is more efficient, they say. Things that happen in 'real time' take too much time. Tethered to technology, we are shaken when that world 'unplugged' does not signify, does not satisfy. After an evening of avatar-to-avatar talk in a networked game, we feel, at one moment, in possession of a full social life and, in the next, curiously isolated, in tenuous complicity with strangers.[110]

---

[110] Sherry Turkle, *Alone Together: Why We Expect More From Technology and Less From Each Other* (New York: Basic Books, 2011), 11.

We have seen in earlier chapters of this book that the human person and humanity as a whole are constantly "in transit," inhabitants of a universe that is created in constant motion, even on the subatomic level. Now, however, human-made technical interventions outdo those of former times and they strike more deeply at the core of what it means to be a human person. There is a fascination in, and a kind of "frenzy for" being the recipient of multiple messages via the social media. Not many people realize how deeply these affect core relationships and the very purpose of life.

Increasingly we are handing-over our interior faculties of thought, will and imagination to outside forces and instruments. These are simultaneously having disembodying, dehumanizing effects, even while they provide instant availability and continuous interconnectedness with others. In fact, there is often a *willingness* to hand over what used to be humanly thought-through and personally chosen, to the guidance of computers and robotic instruments. A simple handy example of this is the familiar "GPS" that reads a car's location and guides its destination through frenetic traffic patterns. On one hand it is a great convenience. On the other it also exemplifies the numerous ways in which the "handing-over" occurs. Satellite-guided directions accustom us to being controlled by inhuman sources that often take on an "ego" and a human-sounding voice.

"Smart homes" are now available. As one upbeat article by Marcus Pickett says: "All of us enjoy the benefits of modern technology even if we're not sure how it all works. The internet, car engines, cell phones: none of it makes complete sense, but we've taken hold of this technology and can no longer live without it."[111] What formerly seemed like something novel in a James Bond film is now being actualized in house design, says Marcus Pickett. Smart Homes are just regular houses except that every piece is hooked up to a computer system and run from a central system so that any device in the home can be a "smart" appliance. Some devices are also connected to manufacturers of household products as well, so that the owner of the house can receive immediate notice of problems and an estimate of repair charges. Pickett says the "real beauty" of this is that one gains more control by giving up control. "In other words, this technology is convenient because smart homes think for themselves."[112]

What's the point of a Smart House? asks Pickett. Absolute convenience. Smart appliances know when they should turn on or off, "know" how much energy they require, and be able to keep up their own maintenance.

---

[111] Marcus Pickett, "Smart Homes Create a Conversation with Your House," https://www.homeadvisor.com/article.show.Smart-Homes-Create-a-Conversation-with-Your-House.14386.html (accessed Feb. 23, 2016).

[112] Pickett, "Smart Homes Create a Conversation with Your House."

"Plus, a computerized house can adapt to the way you live: it knows the time you turn the light on in the morning, it knows what temperature you like your house to stay at, and it even knows when to open the garage door."[113] When you are out of town you can send it a message to make sure that the back burner isn't on and tell the stove that it should turn itself off. Home owners are encouraged to begin investing in smart appliances, gradually building up a home's technology so that owners won't be left behind with the inconveniences of the past.

VIRTUALITY

Within the short space of a few decades, an "imaginary, intangible virtual-reality realm" has permeated practical life. When Michael Heim, sometimes called "the philosopher of cyberspace," wrote of virtual reality in the early 1990's, he noted that the term "virtual reality" is an oxymoron. Formerly, he said, the word "virtual" meant that something was "being in essence or effect though not formally recognized and admitted," while "reality" meant "a real event, entity, or state of affairs." Now, said Heim, "We paste the two together and read: 'Virtual reality is an event or entity that is real in effect but not in fact."[114]

---

[113] Pickett, "Smart Homes Create a Conversation with Your House."

[114] Michael Heim, *The Metaphysics of Virtual Reality* (New York: 1993), 111.

In *The Metaphysics of Virtual* Reality, Heim distinguished seven levels of virtual reality, beginning with **simulation** and moving through **interaction, artificiality, immersion, telepresence, full-body immersion** and **networked communication.** The last of these does not refer to ordinary communication with someone through computer networks, said Heim. He cited Jaron Lanier's saying that it referred to "**post-symbolic communication**" and that it can involve communication "beyond verbal or body language to take on magical, alchemical properties."[115]

Almost twenty years later, in an interview with Diego Rossi, Michael Heim said:

> Nowadays it is difficult to keep a distance from the technologies that we use every day. Our collective culture has pushed everything into the digital. Twenty or thirty years ago, we could sit back and play with virtuality, entertain it as an idea or fantasy. We could be philosophical about the potential of VR for making life more virtual, more fantastic, more magical. That distance – our ability to 'sit back' and contemplate the magic of computing – is now closed..... so

---

[115] See Prokes, *At the Interface: Theology and Virtual Reality*, 13.

we can no longer freely choose to reflect
on computing as one activity among others.
We begin already immersed. That's why we
tend to speak today of 'virtuality' rather
than of 'Virtual Reality.[116]

In the 1980's and 1990's, says Heim, the term "virtual reality" could refer to very specific historical modeling of immersive technology. That has changed and the word "virtuality" is "much broader and covers the manifold ways we are immersed." *Virtuality*, then, has broadened in meaning. While it certainly includes online educational classes, gaming with phantasy football teams, and the construction of imaginary homes in virtual worlds such as "Second Life," it is more encompassing than the discreet programs in which many spend a good portion of daily life. The *environment of virtuality* affects not only the manner in which communication is carried on through technical instruments, but also the way that instantly-available information can be accessed, stored, and scrutinized. This fosters a general uneasiness regarding violations of privacy.

There is a social paradox in this environment: 1) there is a striving for sameness so as "not to be left behind," an attempt to maintain a fragile "social security"; and 2) there

---

[116] Michael Heim, "Virtuality and Dreams [Interview Part I]: Diego Rossi Talking with Michael Heim." www.mheim.com/files/interviewPart1.pdf (accessed Feb. 22, 2016).

is a kind of frantic need for individuals to receive public adulation. The first of these is fed through ubiquitous advertising: possessing the most recent technical items seems to level the social playing field, allowing anyone to "plug-in." The second need is now made possible through public presentations of oneself as an "idol" or celebrity. It is understandable why the word "selfie" has been added to the English vocabulary. How common it is for someone to pull a smart phone from their pocket to display pictures taken with notable performers, politicians, or religious leaders. The desire to be recognized as knowing, or even being near someone famous is not new, but the ways of obtaining that recognition are new.

Sameness can yield boredom and a loss of personal imagination. Airports across the world have a lulling similarity. Their eateries and convenience stores are plastically universal. It would be easy to be confused at times: am I at a departure gate in Rome, Phoenix, or Atlanta? It can be contested what Gertrude Stein precisely meant by saying "There is *no there* there." Many think it was her comment some years ago upon visiting Oakland, California, her hometown. What her observation now means is that something (or someone) lacks its own essence, is vapid. Stein's familiar observation is applicable to malls, online chatter, and sadly, human thought patterns.

Immersed in virtuality, we can swim in it like the proverbial frog, unaware that the water in which it is submerged is being heated more and more until it will be too late to leap out and "review the situation." Sherry Turkle names the kind of restlessness among contemporary young people as life in a "catastrophe culture." Instruments of connection with one another are associated with the dictum: if you receive a call, you are expected to respond because it might be an emergency. "Children are quick to use the term <u>emergency</u> for everything they hope their phones will protect them from," says Turkle. "So many of the young people I spoke with seem to be waiting for an emergency. It could be a personal emergency. But there could be another Katrina, another 9/11. The grid could crash. The story about life as emergencies is about how people, especially young people, develop a fretful self."[117]

CONNECTEDNESS

An article called "Generation C" says of those born after 1990 and who were adolescents after 2000 that they can be termed "Generation C" because they are "connected, communicating, content-centric, computerized, community-oriented, always clicking."[118] There is an expectation

---

[117] Sherry Turkle, *Reclaiming Conversation: The Power of Talk in a Digital Age* ((New York: Penguin Press, 2015), 299.

[118] strategy-business.com, "The Rise of Generation C," http://www. strategy-business.com/article/11110?gko=64e54 (accessed Feb. 23, 2016).

that "Being connected around the clock will be the norm in 2020 – Indeed, it will be a prerequisite for participation in society." It is the first generation to have available from birth an environment defined and enabled by the internet, mobile devices, and networking. "They all have mobile phones, yet they prefer sending text messages to talking with people. More than 95 percent of them have videos on YouTube."[119] Although descriptions may differ somewhat among studies conducted to determine the influence of the virtual milieu on young adults and children, the above description of "Generation C" gives a generalized picture of young adults in countries that have highly-developed technology.

Connectedness is not only a desired goal of children and youths. Having one's Smartphone turned on and close by at all times has become a necessity for people of all ages. The young can feel a quiet panic if their phone is not within reach, if it has been misplaced or turned off. In her person-to-person interviews and research activities with both children and adults, Sherry Turkle has found those interviewed to have a desperate need to keep connected at all times. As noted above, fear and insecurity among the young undergird some of this anxiety to be "technically tethered." Parents, friends, and spouses, however,

---

[119] strategy-business.com, "The Rise of Generation C."

can know the same need to be constantly available to one another and to those who are dependent on their care.

In former times, many children came home from school to a mother or care-giver. Many neighborhoods were havens where children could move about safely, play outdoors together, and not worry about security from human traffickers, drug gangs and child molesters. Now, children are warned to be wary at all times. Some are fearful of coming home to an empty house or of walking through a neighborhood where they feel insecure. It is helpful in these circumstances that a child or teen does have a phone tucked in their pocket or bag to summon help if needed. For many, however, something deeper occurs, and there is an unhealthful dependency on "the connection." It can extend to young adulthood and beyond.

For as social mores change, what once seemed 'ill' can come to seem normal. Twenty years ago, as practicing clinical psychologist, if I had met a college junior who called her mother fifteen times a day, checking in about what shoes to buy and what dress to wear, extolling a certain kind of decaffeinated tea and complaining about the difficulty of a physics problem set, I would have thought her behavior problematic. I would have encouraged her to explore difficulties with separation. I would have assumed that these had to be addressed for her to proceed to successful adulthood. But these days, a college student who texts home fifteen times a day is not unusual.[120]

Even if there are no overt indications of danger, there is among many – adults as well as children – the need to be "turned on" at all times. There is a boundless need for immediacy of receptivity and response. One eighteen-year-old told Turkle that he knows he should not text and drive, but admitted "I know I should, but it's not going to happen. If I get a Facebook message or something posted on my wall....I have to see it. I have to." Several young men told Turkle that they regretted teaching their parents how to text and do IM (instant messaging). Now the parents keep barraging them with messages in order to see how they are doing and what they are doing. Some teenagers argue that they should not be constantly available or "on call" for their parents. Psychologist Turkle underscored the need for teens to have a wholesome separation from their parents – and from each other.

The writer of "The Rise of Generation C" describes "Colin," a computer science student living in London. Twenty years old, he has an interest in backpacking,

---

[120] Turkle, *Alone Together*, 178.

sports, music and gaming. He has a digital device that is connected at all times; he is "connected" wherever he goes. Although close to his family, he prefers to stay in touch with them "virtually through his PDD, which allows him to communicate through multiple channels via voice, text, video, data – either separately or all at once."[121] Although his parents would prefer that he'd visit them more frequently, they are starting to get used to being "part of his digital life." He is part of a generation whose technology is woven into their lives. Fifty-two percent of younger Europeans say that if their mobile phones aren't with them, they feel "disconnected from the world," and ninety-one percent of all mobile phone users "keep their phones within arm's reach, waking or sleeping."[122]

Sometimes comic strips sum up complex matters in a few frames. The comic strip "Zits" features a teen-age boy. One strip pictured him tapping out a text message to his girlfriend who was a short distance from him in the living room. The boy's mother came in, pointed to the girl, and asked why he didn't talk to her since "She's right over there." He looked up and asked "What generation do you come from?"

Family meals used to be centering points, a daily way in which a family stayed connected, where relationships,

---

[121] strategy-business.com, "The Rise of Generation C."

[122] strategy-business.com, "The Rise of Generation C."

activities and difficulties were shared. As food that had been prepared in the family kitchen was eaten, parents and children took in one another and their real life situations. Not only was the body-person nourished at that table: the presence of each member of that family was being offered as gift to the others. The kitchen or dining room table was a place where fears could be allayed through person-to-person sharing, troubling questions brought for problem-solving, and prayers said in times of distress.

In many homes, the dining room table (if there is one) now serves as a catch-all for magazines, back-packs, and electronic paraphernalia. The schedules of family members may vary and often there is but one parent to care for the home, so food is taken hurriedly and individually, or eaten in front of a screen, large or small.

College campuses and dining halls, too, often mirror this lack of person-to-person sharing within families. In the last chapter Sherry Turkle's recent book, *Reclaiming Conversation: The Power of Talk in a Digital Age* was cited, showing the loss of genuine sharing at meals on college campuses. Even though most people probably would not think of keeping the "rule of three," it is important to notice the difficulty of sustaining a conversation among family and friends that treats a subject at some depth. Campfires and long distance drives in a car still offer opportunities for such conversations, but some people get "edgy" when it comes to joining an extended conversation. In Gospel terms, they have "bought a cow, purchased a field or married a wife" and must move on.

A high school senior told Turkle that he's almost always bored. He wants to be "somewhere else," and is almost always texting. He admitted that the possibilities for concentrating are pretty much gone when he's texting, since "You can't focus on the thing you're doing when you are sending the text..... or waiting to receive the text.... there is so much going on with other things you might want to receive on your phone."[123] A far deeper search for connectedness often goes unrecognized. Trying to fill the void, many reach for hand-held instruments that may affirm some connection with others, even with an anonymous person who is also looking for a message.

Pseudo-connections abound across other basic areas of daily life. Financial dealings are conducted electronically apart from the people whose lives are directly concerned in them. Again, this is often taken for granted as a matter of convenience, accuracy and security. For example, financial offerings collected and presented at the Offertory of the Mass, constitute a concrete way of participating in the Holy Sacrifice. These offerings are now often relegated to the business world. There may be generous amounts

---

[123] Turkle, *Reclaiming Conversation*, 214.

allocated for support of the Church, but it is done "from my bank to the parish's bank" as an electronic transaction.

This is not a universal practice among Catholic parishes throughout the world, however. I remember attending a Sunday Mass in Cameroon a few years ago, where three young men made their final profession in a religious community. The parish church could not accommodate the large number of members from each of their tribes, so the tribal members gathered outside the church building. At the Offertory of the Mass, however, the tribes, in turn, entered the Church in procession. Each of the young men led his tribe's procession, with his parents beside him, bringing their offering. Two of those who professed their vows led a goat to present at the foot of the altar. The third offered a live chicken, carried in a mesh bag. Every man, woman and child from a tribe entered the church and with a simple dance step, approached the altar. At its base was a basket into which every person placed whatever bill or coin they brought for an offering. It was a lived experience concerning the meaning of participation in the Eucharistic celebration: personal, peaceful, integral to family worship, and palpable in expression.

DESIRE FOR THE REAL

Although immersed in virtuality, many of our contemporaries are expressing a yearning for the *real* presence of others, and their own personal immersion in real events. They desire to be bodily present for occasions that they value – or for occasions that will make others value them *because* they were present. There is also a longing inherent in the human heart for what is genuine presence that touches the deepest interior of a person, even when they may not be able to explain why.

When this occurs, it can be memorable. A well-known example of this is the desire to be present in St. Peter's Square when "white smoke" comes out of a narrow chimney on the roof of the Sistine Chapel, a delicate natural sign that a new Holy Father has been elected. Many wait for extended periods of time in inclement weather to see if wispy white smoke will emerge from the small chimney. Word spreads quickly once that has been ascertained. Cameras atop St. Peter's Basilica can scope the entire vista below. People come running through all of the streets leading to St. Peter's Square. There is the intense desire to be there *bodily* when the name of the new Pope is announced from the loggia above the basilica's entrance – to *be there* when he emerges into their sight – to *be there* when they hear his voice broadcast over the multitude awaiting his appearance. Anyone present on the early evening of Pope Francis' election, who heard the bells of the Basilica ring, and who saw him emerge almost hesitantly from St. Peter's, will tell you (as if it happened yesterday) what it meant to be present, and to hear his first greeting:

"Bona sera." People do not forget his bowing to them and asking that they bless him.

Key moments of life can still touch humans. Births, marriages, heroic acts, tragedies, and deaths still move people (who may have forgotten how to respond properly to them because they are mostly experienced on hand-held screens from images taken through the lens of a camera). People like to share memories of their presence at significant joyful events or tragedies. Many Americans, for example, are heard to ask one another: *"Where were you* on the morning that 'nine-eleven' happened?"

A surprising phenomenon occurred in the entertainment world between 2011–2016. In cultures saturated with violence and crass television programming, the British historical drama series *Downton Abbey* gained a worldwide audience. Written by Julian Fellowes, who applied meticulous historical accuracy to each segment of the production, the drama portrayed the development of a fictional family from 1912-1925. Superbly acted, the drama followed events of the extended family headed by a "Robert, the Earl of Grantham." Births, marriages, and deaths within a socially privileged family were portrayed and interwoven with those of the hired staff who served the family from the "downstairs" of a Georgian country house. Much of the dramatic series focused on meals, their preparation, and the basic events of life that were celebrated in the mansion amid changing times. Although the historical settings differed greatly from current times, the struggles of growth toward mature love and responsibility were skillfully portrayed as enduring human realities that attracted those who followed the series. Basic truths about humanity endure, and are restlessly delightful when expressed well.

Instead of "humanoid" characters portrayed in virtual unnatural settings, the cast of *Downton Abbey* were actors and actresses who actually expressed a kind of sadness when the series concluded because of the relationships and genuine satisfaction they had known in performing through the series. If the works of Shakespeare were appreciated by the ordinary theater-goers of his day, and retain a lasting meaning across centuries, it may be that the enacted work of Julian Fellowes has expressed a parallel phenomenon in the early twenty-first century.

On the other hand, the *capacity* to recognize and respond to what is of immense significance in one's life can be lost, and a careless shrug replace awe in the presence of what is life-changing. Sherry Turkle writes that we need to ask if it makes us more human to give away our most human jobs. She suggests that it is a time to reconsider the delegation of personal work to machines, not in order to reject technology but "to find" ourselves:

> This is our nick of time and our line to toe: to acknowledge the unintended consequences

of technologies to which we are vulnerable, to respect the resilience that has always been ours. We have time to make the corrections. And to remember who we are – creatures of history, of deep psychology, of complex relationships. Of conversations artless, risky and face-to-face.[124]

In considering how virtuality influences all of life, and contributes to new forms of *restiveness*, it is important to see how deeply the cyber-climate touches identity, bodily reality; and the distinction between invisible realities and imaginary worlds.

IDENTITY

One of the most important questions to ask of another person is "Who are you?" It is also one of the deepest questions to ask of oneself: "Who am I?" As we learn from Jesus Christ, a given name can sometimes indicate a person's mission, or genealogical line, or profound personal identity. Sometimes, a person's identity can also be more fully expressed by several names, each indicating a major characteristic of the person. When Jesus took his apostles to the area of Caesarea-Philippi, he first asked them

---

[124] Turkle, *Reclaiming Conversation: The Power of Talk in the Digital Age*, 362.

"Who do men say that the Son of man is?" (Matt 16:13) but then He asked his Apostles "But who do you say that I am?" (Matt 16:15) Simon said: "You are the Christ, the Son of the living God." (Matt 16:16) In turn, Christ said to Simon: "Blessed are you, Simon Bar-Jonah! For flesh and blood has not revealed this to you, but my Father who is in heaven. And I tell you, you are Peter, and on this rock I will build my church, and the powers of death shall not prevail against it." (Matt 16:17-18)

As noted earlier, true revelation, divine or human, can only be given by persons who *choose* to reveal what could not be found-out, discovered, or scientifically verified by others. Revelation (both divine and human) is only expressed by one who has intimate knowledge and who *chooses* to communicate it. How Jesus must have waited for the Father to reveal the truth of Who He is to a human being, who could then affirm it! Peter himself must have been awed by his ability to pronounce Jesus' Messiah-identity, and further amazed at receiving so precious a mission-identifying name in return. In the Gospel of John, Jesus further speaks his self-identity, especially through His seven "I-am" self-identifications, so intimately connected with the revelation of the divine name to Moses:

I AM the Bread of Life (Jn 6:35)
I AM the Light of the World (Jn 8:12)
I AM the Door of the Sheep (Jn 10:7)

I AM the Good Shepherd (Jn 10:11)

I AM the Resurrection and the Life (Jn 11:25)

I AM the Way, the Truth and the Life (Jn 14:6)

I AM the True Vine (Jn 15:1)

It is noticeable that in recent decades there has been a change in the kinds of names given to children in the United States. Rather than names associated with family members, saints, or heroes, whimsical names associated with colors, seasons, or popular performers are given to children.

The influence of technological programming is important here. Self-identity is precious, but it can now be "distributed" among several or more *personae* associated with electronic games and programs. Twenty years ago, MUD's (Multi-User Dungeons) were what Turkle called "a virtual parlor game and a new form of community."[125] Turkle said that in MUD's the virtual characters could remain anonymous even as they exchanged gestures, conversed or expressed emotions. Not only could characters lose virtual money but also rise and fall socially. This allowed users to express multiple (and often unexpected) aspects of themselves. They could "play with their identity" and "try on" new ones. The MUD's were

---

[125] Sherry Turkle, "Who Am We?" *Wired News*, Issue 4.01, Jan., 1996, http://www.wired.com/wired/archive/4.01/turkle_pr.html (accessed Mar. 12, 2016).

self-authored: "[T]he solitary author is displaced and distributed. Traditional ideas about identity have been tied to a notion of authenticity that such virtual experiences actively subvert..... the self is not only decentered but multiplied without limit."[126] This can bring restive inner confusion.

A flood of films, games, and alternate worlds featured on the Internet have been available since the above MUD possibilities became an attraction. Avatars (icons or figures used to represent oneself in computer-generated forms) have become commonplace. A main feature of an avatar is the possibility of its fashioner to retain anonymity, and to allow an expression of self that would not or could not be identified with the self in real life. This anonymity can create havoc in what were thought to be personal relationships. Altered photos can also be used online for non-existent *personae*, and prove devastating for those who think them to be authentic.

A regrettable example of this was the "real life" experience of Manti Te'o, an outstanding linebacker on Notre Dame University's football team. It became well-known through the media in the college football season of 2011 that tragedy had come to Manti because his grandmother in Hawaii and Lenny Kekua, his girlfriend of several years, had both died within the same week. Manti had "met"

---

[126] Turkle, "Who Am We?"

Lenny Kekua on Twitter. It seemed that they had spoken to one another frequently on the phone. They had never met face-to-face, but Manti had seen her photo on the internet. During that fall's football season, Manti received a telephone call from Lenny in which she told him that she was dying, but she did not want him to come to her funeral. Rather, she said, stay and play very well for Notre Dame in its important game against Michigan. Manti complied with her request.

Several weeks later, however, Manti received a phone call "from Lenny," letting him know that his "relationship" with her had all been a hoax. His grandmother, indeed, had died, but *there was no Lenny Kekua*. A man in California named Ronaiah Tuiasosopo had disguised his voice, making it sound feminine on the phone. He was the person actually calling Manti over several years. From the internet, he had obtained a photo of a real woman, and after altering it, posted it online as "Lenny."

How all of this unfolded over a several-year period remains a tangled account. Television reporters and writers in popular magazines presented conflicting accounts of the relationship between Manti Te'o and his supposed girlfriend. The "Dr. Phil Show" interviewed Manti after the hoax became known, as did American journalist Katie Couric. The puzzling accounts, differing among media outlets, showed a young man, on the way to hero-status, who seemingly trusted the tweets, phone calls and media pictures he had received over a period of time. In a *Vanity Fair* story in 2013, there are comments from Manti Te'o which show his confusion about his personal identity as a public figure, and in his own life. "'My lowest moments were those first days,' he says. 'I just went home, got in bed, and tried to sleep it off so I'd be rested to deal with it. But then, when I went out and around, I could tell people were looking at me. I could hear them whispering and talking about me. And that's when I really started to know how bad this was. And I didn't know what to do with that."[127] Te'o said:

> You have someone you love die. And you find out the person isn't real – that it's all a big prank. You still go through the feelings of losing that person. The relationship, to me, was real. The illness, the accident, her dying – these were all real to me. So my feelings about them were real..... By the time the N.F. L. Combine ended, Te'o said, 'I thought, There, I answered all the questions. It's over.' He says he started feeling something like normal. 'Honestly, I'd say

---

[127] Ned Zeman, "The Man Who Cried Dead Girlfriend," in "VF Culture," *Vanity Fair*, Apr. 25, 2013, http://www.vanityfair.com/culture/2013/06/manti-teo-girlfriend-nfl-draft (accessed Mar. 12, 2016).

I'm never going to be completely normal,'
he says. 'Never. It's still with me now. It's
always going to be something that's just
there all the time, in the back of my head.'[128]

The InternetSociety.org notes that in 1993, when
nobody "knew if you were a dog," users of the internet
felt that they could enjoy a kind of electronic shield of
anonymity. That allowed them to take on any personae
they pleased. Now, web-based industries can keep personal histories that go back more than a decade. "Your
online identity is not the same as your real-world identity because the characteristics you represent online differ
from the characteristics you represent in the physical
world."[129]

Being able to know one's basic identity and to deepen
it throughout life is a precious gift. Soon after Pope Francis
was elected to the papacy, Father Anthony Spadaro, SJ,
conducted an interview of the new Holy Father on behalf
of Jesuit journals throughout the world. His first question to Pope Francis concerned his personal identity, and
it was expressed in terms of his family name. Spadaro
asked: "Who is Jorge Mario Bergoglio?" Spadaro said that

---

[128] Zeman, "The Man Who Cried Dead Girlfriend."

[129] InternetSociety.org, "Understanding your Online Identity: An
Overview of Identity," is-*identityoverview*-20110218-en (accessed
May 9, 2016).

the pope stared at him for a moment, prompting him to ask if that is a question he was allowed to ask. The pope nodded and then said:

> I do not know what might be the most fitting description..... I am a sinner. This is the most accurate definition. It is not a figure of speech, a literary genre. I am a sinner'.....Yes, perhaps I can say that I am a bit astute, that I can adapt to circumstances, but it is also true that I am a bit naïve. Yes, but the best summary, the one that comes more from the inside and I feel most true is this: I am a sinner whom the Lord has looked upon.[130]

The surprise of Spadaro's opening question required an immediate kind of transparency of Pope Francis, a vulnerability that resonates with Arthur Vogel's description of body-meaning cited in the previous chapter, where he says that body-meaning has to do with a personal presence that anchors us in the world. This allows a person to mean what they say and say what they mean, commonly expressed as the ability to "stand behind our words."

---

[130] Anthony Spadaro, "A Big Heart Open to God," http://americamagazine.org/pope-interview (accessed Mar. 13, 2016).

PORNOGRAPHY

Pope Francis' self-identification is the antithesis of a kind of virtual anonymity which invites untruthfulness and the use of pornography in the social media. Although discussed briefly in the previous chapter as a cause of acrid restiveness in the present world, pornography must be recognized here again within the context of cyberspace. Pornography, a multi-billion dollar industry, is not only readily available throughout multiple forms of the media. It is foisted upon those who detest it, but are unable to block every avenue of its tentacles within the instruments of communication. It is evident not only in dark backrooms, "adult" book and film stores, but is blatantly woven into advertising, entertainment and education. In their Pastoral Letter in response to pornography, the United States Conference of Catholic Bishops spoke of the cultural pervasiveness of pornography. Although pornography is not new, they stated that the Church always has the need to scrutinize the signs of the times. The instant availability of this scourge is a particularly dark side of the cyber-laced world. The Bishops point out the connections that pornography has with sex trafficking and commercial sexual exploitation worldwide.[131]

---

[131] See USCCB Committee on Laity, Marriage, Family Life and Youth of the United States, "Create in Me a Clean Heart: A Pastoral Response to Pornography Use," #4, issued Nov. 15, 2015.

Among the statistics on the production and use of Internet Pornography are these: twelve percent of all websites on the internet are pornographic, amounting to 24,644,172 sites. Forty million Americans are regular visitors to porn sites. Thirty-five percent of all internet downloads are pornographic, and two and a half billion emails per day are also pornographic.[132] Already in 2013, the *Huffington Post* carried this message: "The Internet is for porn. We all know that, but until now we may not have realized to what extent porn dominated the Internet..... In fact, 30 percent of all data transferred across the Internet is porn.[133]

These statistics do not record the devastating kinds of restiveness that afflict those who have fallen into habits of pornographic viewing or are addicted to it. It is impossible to measure how many lives have been severely charred by being enslaved and/or trafficked in the porno trade. Some have willingly participated in performing/filming/producing what degrades not only them, but all who will view what they portray. Rodney Pelletier writes that sixty-four percent of video porn is watched on cell phones or

---

[132] Michael Smalley, "You have no idea ....the world and statistics of pornography," http://www.smalley.cc/idea-world-statistics-pornography/ (accessed Mar. 13, 2016).

[133] "Porn Sites Get More Visitors Each Month Than Netflix, Amazon and Twitter combined," *The Huffington Post*, May 4, 2013, http://www.huffingtonpost.com/2013/05/03/internet-porn-stats_n_3187682. (accessed Mar. 13, 2016).

tablets, an increase of close to 18 percent between 2014 and January of 2016.[134] The number of pornography consumers among women is rising. Pornographic images and actions have been with humanity over millennia, but never have there been so many possibilities of viewing and participating in it.

Personal evil is real and distorts what is good. C. S. Lewis in his *Screwtape Letters* has an experienced devil instruct a devil-in-training how to tempt humans at their weakest points. The very instruments that allow more time for recreation and greater access to what can be hidden from others (even during professional work hours) present a passel of "weak points" open to temptation and deceit. The adage is verified: the corruption of the best is the worst. The tools of technology which hold great potential for unifying the human community and providing for basic human needs can destroy with a particular ferocity when infiltrated by evil.

The positive use of electronic instruments is overshadowed often by the irresponsible use of media sources which can shatter personal identity, destroy relationships, and degrade human persons. On the other hand, the media can provide opportunities for new forms of

---

[134] Rodney Pelletier, "Global porn use increases to record highs – approaching 10 billion hours," ChurchMilitant.com, Jan. 17, 2016, http://churchmilitant.com/news/article/2015-porn-stats-show-alarming (accessed May 9, 2016).

conversation and evangelization. Just as the internet and telephone were used to con and deceive a young athlete at the height of his college football career, they can be used positively to assist others in initially receiving and then sustaining the truths of faith and shared prayer. Televised Masses, prayer services and varied informative programs are very helpful to those who are homebound or under care in institutional settings. Multiple "apps" are available, making it possible for those in remote parts of the earth to receive the truths of faith and participate in spirit with members of the Church in far-away countries, but the virtues of chastity and temperance are essential in protecting the wonders of technology from being instruments of destruction and the loss of inner peace.

TRANSHUMANISM

Since the middle of the last century there have been concerted efforts by "futurists" to hasten a time when humans will surpass the limited powers of interior faculties and the natural limitations inherent in being in-the-body. Technical and scientific means to achieve this are moving ever more swiftly. As explained in an article cited in Chapter I: "The Future is Coming Much Faster than You Think," technological advances are no longer happening in a *linear* fashion, but *exponentially*. Until recently, linear ways of measuring change worked well.

Now, however, change is happening exponentially, not in a linear sequence.

> Many studies have tracked the advances of many different measures of information technology, and have identified that performance (in relation to price) doubles on average every 18 months. As the rate of our advance continues to accelerate, the future continues to come faster than we traditionally expect.

> When graphing exponential growth, we eventually reach a point where growth seems 'vertical.' This stage of growth is often referred to as the Technological Singularity..... It is a time that seems incomprehensible, and will be possible through our creating sentient Artificial Intelligence, which will have intelligence level (sic) far superior to our own.[135]

With exponential advances, there is – and will be magnified restlessness, spurring us to surpass the limitations of the human body-person through the genius of technical

---

[135] "The Future is Coming Much Faster than we Think, Here's Why."

enhancement. Elements of films and e-games that once were part of science fiction have already been realized. These focus on the merging of humans with technical instruments in order (at least temporarily) to *enhance* the bodies and intellects of humans so that within decades, these instruments may surpass their human inventors.

Robotic vacuum cleaners and delivery carts are now routinely utilized in carrying out mundane tasks that humans find burdensome or boring. Assembly plant robots have "laser eyes" that fit parts into automobiles with a precision and consistency that make them not only efficient but very accurate. Beyond the usefulness of such practical robots there is competition among companies to fashion robots that take on *seeming* aspects of human interactions, including emotional responses. As pointed out earlier in this book, robotic pets have been on the market for some time but are now increasingly anticipated as *companions* both children and elders. Sherry Turkle says that children imagine sociable robots as substitutes for the persons who are missing in their lives.

In the summer of 2015 the first "robot wedding" was held in Japan. One hundred Japanese paid eighty-one dollars each to attend. The robot representing the bride was formed to resemble a female's body, but the robot form of the supposed groom was fashioned with the more usual robot characteristics, with tube-arms and antennas. There was a robot band at the wedding and snacks for the humans who attended. It is predicted that marriage between a human and a robot will take place before long. A sixteen-year-old girl told Sherry Turkle that while she considered having a robot for a friend, it wasn't for her but she could at least understand why it would have an appeal. People try to make friends but don't succeed. "So when they hear this idea about robots being made to be companions, well, it's not going to be like a human and have its own mind to walk away or leave you or anything like that. Relationship-wise, you're not going to be afraid of a robot cheating on you, because it's a robot. It's programmed to stay with you forever."[136]

The planning and highly technical experimentation regarding human/machine projects go much further. A "cyborg" is a person whose physical tolerance or capabilities are extended beyond normal human limitations and whose bodily functions are modified. How long ago the characters in early sci-fi novels, films, and "comic books" portrayed heroes and heroines who exceeded ordinary human knowledge, mobility, and strength. There has long been a restlessness to achieve in real life what the imagination seeks. The urge to overcome barriers continues, but the goals of transhumanists and posthumanists fuel the exponential advances of the digital age in ever-new ways. Ray Kurzweil predicts that the "Singularity" will

---

[136] Turkle, *Reclaiming Conversation*, 350-351.

be reached by 2045, although others involved in this stretch toward the future think it will take more time. Kurzweil writes:

> The Singularity – technological change so rapid and profound it represents a rupture in the fabric of human history. The implications include the merge of biological and nonbiological intelligence, immortal software-based humans, and ultra-high levels of intelligence that expand outward in the universe at the speed of light.[137]

Kurzweil thinks that humanity won't experience just 100 years of progress in the 21st century, but 20,000 years of "progress." Plans to scan the brain are neither science fiction in scope, nor intended simply to gain understanding of the human mind. The plan is to scan a person's brain in order to download it, and "reinstantiate their personal mind file into a suitable computing medium."[138] Kurzweil goes on to say that the downloaded "person" will seem to observers to have very much the same personality, history

---

[137] Ray Kurzweil, "The Law of Accelerating Returns," Mar. 7, 2001, http://www.kurzweilai.net/the-law-of-accelerating-returns (accessed Feb. 28, 2016).

[138] Kurzwweil, "The Law of Accelerating Returns."

and memory as the person whose brain was originally scanned.

Of course, this transfer from person to machine involves disembodiment and touches the meaning of immortal life. Kurzweil admits that many think the placing of a human mind into a computational medium requires the provision of a body of some kind. He does not find that impossible. A body could be built atom by atom, he says, or built through nanotechnology: *virtual bodies that exist only in virtual reality.* He offers an alternative: an enhancement of a person's biological brain through gene enhancement or replacement, able to be modified later by nanotechnology.

Some think that nanotechnology, the manipulation of matter on a molecular scale, will have a spectacular break-through in the near future, evoking great competition and a struggle to control world economies. Governments have already invested billions of dollars for experimentation in nanotechnology. It is projected that great numbers of extremely small nano-machines will be injected into the human body, for example, in order to combat diseases. The implications of nanotechnical experimentation and its applications are hardly recognized yet, but billions of people who will be either benefitted or harmed by them.

Speaking from a faith perspective, Rebecca Taylor has written that most people in the fast-paced world are totally unaware of the dangerous philosophy of transhumanism.[139] She describes transhumanism as envisioning a world where humans can leave behind both ignorance and weak existence. Individuals can enhance their way to becoming supersmart, superstrong, superhappy, basically superhuman. The goal is to create a new species – posthumans – where human limitations, including death, are no more. Taylor refers to Ray Kurzweil's prediction that we won't be satisfied to just *use* cellphones and computers, but will integrate them bodily. She describes what Kurzweil thinks "human-body version. 2.0" will be like:

> [M]ostly 'non-biological, where nanobots replace our heart, lungs, nervous and digestive systems. The enhanced human 2.0 could run an 'Olympic sprint for 15 minutes without taking a breath,' eat anything and never get fat, have superintelligence and create any virtual reality, including a virtual lover, inside the nervous system at will. And most importantly to Kurzweil, the human 2.0 will never die.[140]

---

[139] See Rebecca Taylor, "Transhumanism Taking the Place of Our Creator," *National Catholic Register*, Nov. 18 – Dec. 1, 2012.

[140] Rebecca Taylor, "Transhumanism: Taking the Place of Our Creator," ncregister.com, http://www.register.com/site/article/transhumanism-yaking-the-place-of-ou (accessed May 9, 2016).

Taylor cites Kyle Munkittrick whose "Seven Conditions for Attaining Transhumanism" appeared in *Discover Magazine.* "One condition is we leave the traditional ideas about humanity behind and reject being human as a prerequisite for personhood. Munkittrick writes, 'When African grey parrots, gorillas and dolphins have the same rights as a human toddler, a transhuman-friendly rights system will be in place.'"[141]

A major factor in the development of the instruments and machines discussed above, is "AI" or Artificial Intelligence. It is not only persons of faith who are concerned about ongoing experimentation and the development of Artificial Intelligence. An *Observer* opinion article reported the concerns of eminent scientists and technologists:

> 'Success in creating AI would be the biggest event in human history,' wrote Stephen Hawking in an op-ed, which appeared in *The Independent* in 2014. 'Unfortunately, it might also be the last, unless we learn how to avoid the risks'..... Mr. Hawking recently joined Elon Musk, Steve Wozniak, and hundreds of others in issuing a letter unveiled at the International Joint Conference last

---

[141] Taylor, "Transhumanism: Taking the Place of Our Creator."

month in Buenos Aires, Argentina. The
letter warns that artificial intelligence
can potentially be more dangerous than
nuclear weapons.[142]

There is a head-long rush on the part of some futurists
to exceed any limitation on what the creative mind can
project and what technical skill and scientific knowledge
can deliver. This is a kind of restiveness that challenges
all humanity at the present moment and invites intense
prayer, earnestly asking that the Holy Spirit increase His
gifts and our receptivity of them.

Lemmings do leap off cliffs into the sea, and those that
survive the fall keep swimming onward out to sea, as if
there is a place to land. They are still an apt metaphor for
non-acceptance of realities that exceed human calculation,
pressing onward, defying all boundaries, pushing at the
limits of what it means to be an embodied person destined for eternal life with Divine Persons. The gift of life-
deep restlessness for personal love and self-gift cannot
be satiated by a ruthless flinging of self beyond human
limitations.

---

[142] observer.com, "Stephen Hawking, Elon Musk, and Bill Gates Warn
About Artificial Intelligence" http://observer.com/2015/08/
stephen-hawking-elon-musk-and-bill-gates-warn-about-artificial-
intelligence (accessed Mar.15, 2016).

Chapter V

WAITING, SUFFERING: RESTLESSNESS WITHIN

How do we wait for God? We wait with patience. But patience does not mean passivity. Waiting patiently is not like waiting for the bus to come, the rain to stop, or the sun to rise. It is an active waiting in which we live the present moment to the full in order to find there the signs of the One we are waiting for..... Waiting patiently always means paying attention to what is happening before our eyes and seeing there the first rays of God's glorious coming.[143]

---

[143] Henri Nouwen, "Waiting with Patience," Henri Nouwen Society, http://henrinouwen.org/meditation/waiting-with-patience/ (accessed Mar. 31, 2016).

hree times within the twentieth chapter of his Gospel, John writes of the Risen Christ's Easter greeting: "Peace be with you." Jesus appeared in the midst of disciples gathered behind "shut doors" and said "Peace be with you." (Jn 20:19) After showing them His hands and side, "Jesus said to them again 'Peace be with you.'" (Jn 20: 21) Eight days later, when Thomas was present with the other apostles, "The doors were shut, but Jesus came and stood among them, and said, 'Peace be with you.'" (Jn 20:26) It is Jesus' Easter message to a small band who were frightened, bewildered, and resistant to belief. It was the same divine Person who, in vulnerable flesh, had told them not to be afraid as He walked toward them on a thrashing sea – yet, whose own "sweat became like great drops of blood falling upon the ground" (Lk 22:44) when He knew agony in the Garden of Gethsemane. The peace given by Christ does not comprise a facile escape from anxiety, limitation, and sorrow. His peace emanates from relationship with the Father and the Holy Spirit.

Christ-peace is a holy paradox: there may be inner terror and instability underfoot, but also a certainty of the divine presence that holds all in love. It is the mystery of "still and still moving" brought to bear among the swiftly-moving events of ordinary life, and divine interventions that interrupt what had been humanly planned. Christ-peace is a holy restlessness that is open to *waiting, limitation, suffering, death* – and *surprise*.

The events of the first Easter exemplify this in enduring ways. They were not tidy, or humanly pre-programmed. Grieving women rose in darkness to prepare spices for a beloved's crucified body. At dawn, they hastened with their burden to a tomb whose stone covering was rolled back to reveal a gaping entrance. Messengers in white robes told them that the one they sought had risen, he was not there. They hurried to inform mourning disciples of the incredible news. Peter and John raced to the tomb, and distraught Mary Magdalene mistook her "Rabboni" for a gardener. Guards panicked on discovering that their watch had been disrupted and they hastened to their superiors with news that could have meant their death.

In all, the first Easter Day was one of improbabilities, of undignified running to and fro, of confusion sliced through with unpredictable joy! The event that divided all human life – indeed, all creation – into before and after, did not happen with accolades and trumpet blasts on the Temple steps, and stars falling from the sky like spring rain, but with scurrying feet, disbelief, even terror among those who expected familiar procedures following tragedy.

Easter morning would have been the first workday of the week for many in Jerusalem. Donkeys laden with produce and rare spices from the East would have struggled beneath their burdens along the Way of the Cross that Jesus had traversed three days earlier. Merchants would have haggled with their customers over the price of a choice cut of meat and tax collectors would have insisted on a hefty payment. On a day that seemed "business as usual" in Jerusalem, the Future of human life and meaning moved serenely but unexpectedly among the distraught and the happily amazed.

Patient with human incredulity, the Risen Savior walked on a country road outside Jerusalem, interpreted the meaning of salvation history for two of his disconcerted disciples, and broke bread with them to reveal His identity. Then, he appeared in the midst of the men who had shared the Last Supper with Him, and requested a bit of broiled fish to make them understand that it was Himself, not a ghost who came unbidden through their locked door. He came with a greeting of peace into a milieu turned upside down from ordinary "peace."

Should we be amazed that when we wake to a new day we do not know what will transpire before we sleep again? Although we have been told that God's Ways are not our ways, and that we do not think as God does, we persist in efforts to control the universe, to steady our feet, irrespective of the fact that we are swirling and traveling at mind-boggling speeds in a universe minutely held in place by gravity: all this, despite being "rationally" aware that we really don't know the day nor the hour when we will be greeted by the Risen Lord's summons to come Home. Perhaps we could not put one foot in front of another if we remembered that "intentionally" at all times.

Peace is not the cessation of movement, but the "still and still moving" of love's response to the restlessness of life in its multiple dimensions. Blogger Michael Webb says:

> In the most private spaces of each person's inner conscious life, a deep dissatisfaction is lurking, a nagging sense that life is somehow out of kilter, misaligned, not quite as it should be..... Nothing in the physical world ever lines up exactly with our inner concepts. How we respond to the experience of that misalignment is what matters.[144]

If events large and small did *not* change, they would also be distressing. Sunsets, for example, are associated with peace, and bring calm. If they suddenly remained immobile, however, they would lose their soothing effect. It is the seeming merge of sun with field or sea, and the blend of changing light and color that bring delight. A contemplative nun in the northeastern United States described the splendor of a winter morning's hoarfrost that etched every twig, thistle and fence-line under a blue sunlit sky. In an hour, the sun would melt the white coat of frost. The nun said how wistful she had been at times,

---

[144] Michael Webb, "The Root Cause of Human Suffering," Apr., 2006, www.sklatch.net/thoughtlets/dukkha.html (accessed Mar. 31, 2016).

desiring the white grandeur to remain under the brilliant sky, until she realized: "It was as if God said, 'Now, that was lovely. Let's see what else we should try.'"

There can be an unwholesome cessation of change, an unwillingness to let go what is good and treasured so that something greater could be realized. The resurrected Lord had to tell Mary Magdalene "Do not hold me, for I have not yet ascended to the Father; but go to my brethren and say to them, I am ascending to my Father and your Father, to my God and your God." (Jn 20:17) Attempts to make "still life" of what we value and possess leads to deadly stagnancy and can deprive them of the development of their potential.

We are not made for permanence in this world. Yet, to steady self in the midst of change, and attain equilibrium, we can flail about, trying to control not only ourselves, but others and the world about us. The truth is that we are always "on the way" toward a destination that exceeds our finest planning and ability to control. In the previous chapter of this book, it was explained that gifted scientists and technical experts are attempting to secure a future that throbs with exhilarating plans to *exceed* human limitations. What is promised in such a future is *indefinite human life* technically confined in the present material universe. Reality in God, instead, outstrips our imaginings, and pervasive restlessness is a gift that accompanies our *waiting, and our way of responding to limitation, resistance to boundaries, and suffering.*

WAITING

A distinction can be made between anticipation and waiting. Anticipation can be either a time of joy and excitement, or a dread of what threatens to harm or destroy. It is the "in-between" time that separates the present moment and some future occurrence still uncertain in its particulars. There can be a kind of playful fear that things will not turn out as well as one hopes (children, for example, know this kind of apprehension when taken to visit Santa Clause in the local shopping mall; adults, holding a narrow paper printout, anticipate being a winner in the random selection of numbers for a multi-million-dollar lottery prize). At various times in life, anticipation can take on great seriousness, but it is usually of shorter duration than *waiting.*

Waiting pervades the mystery of human life. As Henri Nouwen emphasized, waiting has two aspects: "One is the waiting for God, and the other is the waiting of God. We are waiting. God is waiting."[145] Nouwen describes the opening scene of the Good News as filled with waiting people who in some way hear "Do not be afraid. I have

---

[145] Henri Nouwen, "A Spirituality of Waiting," an article condensed from a tape available from Ave Maria Press, Notre Dame, Indiana 46556.

something good to say to you."[146] *Waiting* is revealed as an essential element of divine intent and action in creation. It is an element of love, and concludes with the spectacular restlessness described in the Book of Revelation, what is "yet to come." Sometimes waiting involves small matters. At other times, fidelity in waiting involves matters that have life-changing, world-changing significance – but they can relate to seemingly small and non-important measures.

The persons and events of Scripture are steeped in holy waiting. The opening chapter of Genesis unfolds in a series of "days" that await a culmination in the creation of Adam and Eve in the image of God, followed by a divine "resting" on the seventh day. As noted earlier in Augustine's prayer, humanity is created *toward* God, constituting a mutual waiting in love, a basic theme of both Old and New Testaments. Robert McMahon writes:

> The best-known sentence in the *Confessions* comes in its first chapter and epitomizes Augustine's understanding of human nature. The praying speaker acknowledges that God stirs human beings to delight in praising him, 'because thou hast made us toward thyself and our heart is restless

---

[146] Nouwen, "A Spirituality of Waiting."

184

until it rests in thee'..... by our very nature we are drawn toward God. That is why the human heart is 'restless' amidst all the goods of the created world..... human beings are made by and for Someone..... Hence the Augustinian heart has both an incompleteness, for it is 'restless,' and a directionality toward God.[147]

The persons and events of Scripture are steeped in holy waiting. At the most solemn moments of life and human history, the inner intensity of waiting is expressed and often ritualized outwardly in enduring ways. The directives "to watch, to wait, and be vigilant" are woven through the sacred words of Scripture like a symphonic theme. Note how it was at the Tree of Life in the Garden that a covenant of future salvation was announced. It would be fulfilled only after a long time of waiting, when the "hour had come" for Jesus, Son of the Creating Father, to be hung on another Tree of Life, on Calvary. Waiting is the joy/pain woven through the history of salvation. Even in the most desperate of situations, waiting is the love-sign of covenantal hope, and it is difficult.

---

[147] Robert McMahon, "Augustine's Confessions and Voegelin's Philosophy," (*MA 48:1, Winter, 2006) – 12/09/08*, in *First Principles*, ISI Web Journal, Mar. 21, 2016, 1.

Psalm 2:4 has a rare reference to God's "laughter," but in the seriousness of fidelity to waiting there can also be a divine humor. How else could we explain human delight in humor, made as we are in the image of the creator? At God's command, Noah prepared an ark (humanly implausible in its size and purpose). Then he waited through the tedious stretches of rain and flood, and the subsiding of the waters. Only after a dove that he sent forth from the ark returned to him – "and lo, in her mouth a freshly plucked olive leaf" (Gen.8:11) – did Noah, his family and the animals emerge from the ark. Noah was given the sign of a covenantal rainbow in the clouds, and offered sacrifice. For his faithful waiting, he and his family became a new beginning of humanity. **Improbability** according to human reckoning is a mark of divine activity in creation and divine personal love-gift. The First Letter of St. Peter, included in the Office of Readings for Friday of Easter Week, says:

> For Christ also died for sins once for all,
> the righteous for the unrighteous, that he
> might bring us to God, being put to death
> in the flesh but made alive in the spirit; in
> which he went and preached to the spirits
> in prison, who formerly did not obey, when
> God's patience waited in the days of Noah,
> during the building of the ark, in which a few,
> that is, eight persons, were saved through

water. Baptism, which corresponds to this,
now saves you....(I Pet 3: 18-21)

Peter writes of the patient waiting of God and how it
touches back through millennia even to Noah and covenantal fidelity. To be patient is to bear well the chafing of
waiting. For Noah it meant waiting for the waters to sub-
side. For us? Patience in human love responds to God who
waits in merciful love. For us, however, extended patience
is painful. There is a restlessness in waiting that pulls at
the raw hem of our thought and tugs at the ragged edge
of our impatience.

Throughout the Hebrew Testament, the Books of
Judges, Prophets and Kings, there is the persistent call
sealed in covenants: **wait**. Earlier in this book we pondered on Abraham and Sarah. On a simmering midday, as
Abram sat at the door of his tent, three visitors arrived
and received hospitality. They told of an unthinkable
happening still to unfold: the patriarch and his wife Sarai
would conceive a child in the coming year. In terms of
waiting, the couple seemingly were nearing the conclu-
sion of a long but sterile marriage. It was but one of many
startling instances of the divine pattern in the history of
salvation: on the cusp of seeming failure or hopelessness,
divine fruitfulness is given. There would be no substitute:
in this case, trying to obtain a child of promise and destiny through a servant would not replace the gift of a child

naturally conceived in marriage beyond ordinary child-bearing years.

This pattern of divine assistance in conceiving new life after a time of faithful waiting recurs in the inspired Word of God. For example, year after year, Hannah lamented her barrenness and pleaded with God for a child. Only in their advanced years was the child Samuel granted to her and Elkanah. Not only was the child conceived in their old age, but he became one of the great prophets of Israel. Elizabeth and Zechariah were recognized as "walking in all the commandments and ordinances of the Lord blameless" and yet had no child "because Elizabeth was barren, and both were advanced in years." (Lk 1:6-7) When Zechariah as priest was fulfilling his service of burning incense in the temple, an angel of the Lord appeared to him, telling him that not only would Elizabeth's prayer be heard in bearing a son, but the child would "be filled with the Holy Spirit, even from his mother's womb," would go before God in "the spirit and power of Elijah" and "make ready for the Lord a people prepared." (Lk 1:15, 17)

In the history of salvation, the striking circumstances surrounding the birth of significant children from elder parents complements the birth of the Son of God who was conceived in the womb of the young virgin Mary – not as a result of urgent request, but as unanticipated gift. God is the giver of life. It is not agitation and frantic human achievement that accomplish the plans hidden in the heart of God from all eternity. Scripture shows graphically the sacredness of human life: no phase of development, no age of life lacks deep significance.

In both old and young, however, a keen restlessness accompanies those who trust in the Lord. The elder Hannah, for example, yearned, pleaded with God, and wept for a child. Zechariah even disbelieved the reality when promised that Elizabeth would conceive. He asked Archangel Gabriel "How shall I know this?" (Lk 1: 18) Mary's response to Gabriel's message was not how she would *know*, but how it was to *be*. In other words, the conception of the Son of God would not happen through ordinary marital relations and she needed to know what was asked of her. She was "greatly troubled" by the angel's greeting and received assurance: "Do not be afraid, Mary, for you have found favor with God." (Lk 1:30)

The profound rightness of truth and peace does not exempt one from a holy restlessness. Overshadowed by the Holy Spirit and bearing the God-man within her body, Mary would still come to know that a divine Father would permit His Son to be laid, shivering, in an animal's manger. The young mother would hear Simeon's prophecy that a sword of sorrow would pierce her heart, and she would learn in the darkness of night to rise and flee, and that her newborn Son was the reason for Herod's slaying innocent babes.

St. Augustine in a Treatise on Psalm 54:1 says: "Hear, O God, my prayer, and despise not my supplication: be attentive to me and hear me. These are the words of a man in trouble, of one in anxiety, and set in tribulation. He prays in his great sufferings, longing to be rid of his affliction."[148] The psalmist will have to tell us what his affliction is, Augustine says, but "It remains for us to see in what affliction he may be: and when he shall begin to tell us, let us recognize ourselves in it; so that communion in suffering may bring about union in prayer."[149] The psalmist says a wicked man is causing this suffering, a form of grief and affliction that the psalmist terms his "exercise." Augustine then relates this to the truth that nothing happens without purpose. "Do not think that wicked men are in this world for nothing," he said, "or that God does no good with them. Every wicked man lives, either to repent, or to exercise the righteous."[150]

Teresa of Calcutta, saint of service to the dying poor, made known that the greatest trial of her life was the darkness of God's seeming distance from her over several decades of her life, while she personally consoled the bereft and founded religious communities. Father

---

[148] Saint Augustine, Lesson IV, of *Tenebrae* for Good Friday, trans. in text prepared for Franciscan Sisters of the Eucharist, Meriden, Connecticut, 14-15.

[149] Augustine, Lesson IV, 15.

[150] Augustine, Lesson IV, 15.

Kolodiejchuk, member of the Missionaries of Charity family, said:

> Although the Albanian nun is always seen beaming and smiling brightly in photos, she experienced a profound internal desolation during which she felt silence and rejection from God, who seemed distant.

> In a letter to her spiritual director in 1957, Mother Teresa wrote that 'I call, I cling, I want, and there is no one to answer. When I try to raise my thoughts to heaven, there is such convicting emptiness that those very thoughts return like sharp knives and hurt my very soul.'

> 'Love – the word – it brings nothing. I am told God lives in me – and yet the reality of darkness and coldness and emptiness is so great that nothing touches my soul,' she said.[151]

---

[151] Elise Harris, "Mother Teresa was heroic – but maybe not for the reasons you think," catholicnewsagency.com, http://www. catholicnewsagency.com/news/mother-teresa-was-heroic-but-ma (accessed Apr. 6, 2016).

Holy waiting is vigilance, a "being awake" to the coming of God in the midst of life's habitual events, and in the surprises that pierce ordinary expectations with joy or pain or terror. Each new day is like a condensed lifetime, unopened in its dawning, pieced together by the routine and the unexpected. Much of it is spent waiting, but not in heroic ways. It may include waiting for the last child to leave for school, backpack slung into place; or waiting in line for the grocery packer; or for the office staff to assemble; or for the dish washer to complete its cycle; for a spouse to come home; or for Mass to begin. These are the stuff of parables, home, and marketplaces. Jesus' parables focused on the significance of watching and waiting, whether one is in the middle of duties, terror bombs, or "elevator music."

Jesus cautioned servants entrusted with care of their master's property to be watchful – not only for what has been placed in their care, but for the return of their master. Luke writes of Christ's parable of the master returning from his wedding feast:

> Let your loins be girded and your lamps
> burning, and be like men who are waiting
> for their master to come home from the
> marriage feast, so that they may open to him
> at once when he comes and knocks. Blessed
> are those servants whom the master finds

awake when he comes; truly, I say to you, he will gird himself and have them sit at table, and he will come and serve them. If he comes in the second watch, or in the third, and finds them so, blessed are those servants. (Lk 12:35-38)

The wise and foolish virgins were told to watch for the coming of the bridegroom with their lamps lit (Matt 25:1-13). To be alert, on the *"qui vive,"* is a restless sign of love – seeking the beloved who might appear at any moment. The *Song of Songs* graphically portrays the intense restlessness of the beloved's search for the beloved.

To watch and wait in Christ requires a sacred reading of the times: to know when to let-go of control in the "Noah-an" sense – not only to torrents of rain and floods, but to the delicacy of God's message in a fresh olive leaf delivered in the beak of a dove. The "narrator" in Nikos Kazantzakis' *Zorba the Greek* tells with remorse in adult years of an incident from his youth when he showed intemperate restlessness. He had discovered a cocoon on the bark of a tree. A butterfly had made a hole in the cocoon and was slowly preparing to emerge:

I waited awhile, but it was too long appearing and I was impatient. I bent over it and breathed on it to warm it. I warmed it as quickly as I could and the miracle began to happen before my eyes, faster than life. The case opened; the butterfly started slowly crawling out, and I shall never forget my horror when I saw how its wings were folded back and crumpled; the wretched butterfly tried with its whole trembling body to unfold them. Bending over it, I tried to help it with my breath, in vain. It needed to be hatched out patiently and the unfolding of the wings should be a gradual process in the sun. Now it was too late.[152]

To hasten what needs its "hour" is to destroy. The narrator in Kazantzakis' novel averred "For I realize today that it is a mortal sin to violate the great laws of nature. We should not hurry, we should not be impatient, but we should confidently obey the eternal rhythm."[153]

BOUNDARIES

Many of the world's regional/national (and particularly well-financed) populations are moving forward at reckless exponential speed, finding it difficult to be

---

[152] Nikos Kazantzakis, *Zorba the Greek*, trans Carl Wildman (New York: Simon and Schuster, 1952), 121.

[153] *Zorba the Greek,"* p. 121.

restrained by limitations. This applies to legal limits, but even more extensively to the natural limitations of the human body and interior personal faculties, to natural law relationships in the human family, and to the exquisitely precise created forces operative in the universe.

Evidence of the press against any limitation is expressed in ordinary areas of human endeavor. In cultures sustained with an abundance of life's needs and comforts, and where physical work is being replaced by technical and mechanical instruments, there are strong efforts to exceed both human and technical boundaries.

Within human limitations there is also the drive to exceed what has been done before, and as St. Paul knew, the desire to compete and discipline one's body so as to "win the wreath" was worthy of imitation for a greater cause. Compare the speed, coordination, and precision of basketball teams today with those of forty years ago. Players are honed in their intake of food, their capacity to lift weights, to run and to handle the objects of their sport in ways not possible a few decades ago. Indy and NASA car drivers race machines at speeds and distances not possible in previous times. Skiers, bobsledders, and triathlon athletes prepare to set new world records, to break through former limits in their sport. Young "Icarus roller-bladers" soar sunward above the edges of their half-tubes in death-defying moves.

Advertisers show a cascade of exploding, fiery and violent images accompanied by persons or animated characters screaming, rapping, and catapulting to high decibel sounds in order to sell simple products, hoping that their disjointed mélange of image, noise (and often absurd or sexually-ramping) messages will evoke a desire for their product. To be more daring in *over-riding limitations* in dress and suggestive language is an evident goal of advertising personnel attempting to bring attention to a product or service.

These are indicative of the desire to surpass the boundaries of natural and/or legal limits. Morally, a sexual and marital revolution that began in the 1960's has come full circle. Pope Paul VI, in issuing his encyclical *Humanae Vitae*, said prophetically that once the natural and sacred sexual realities of love-giving and life-giving in marriage were breached, every aberration would be possible. That has occurred. How swiftly the United States and other nations have abolished respect for natural gender and sexual identities. Analogically, it's as if a bomb has leveled every boundary of human identity. Individuals can stand in the barren ashes, leveled in all directions toward bleak and colorless moral horizons, open to the prevailing winds coming from any shifting direction. Often, across this destruction there is wailing to the a-rhythmic gyrations of an increasingly-mechanized body the cry of being "free at last!"

Father Ronald Rolheiser writes in *The Holy Longing*:

> It is no easy task to walk the earth and find
> peace. Inside of us, it would seem, some-
> thing is at odds with the very rhythm of
> things and we are forever restless, dissatis-
> fied, frustrated, and aching. We are so over-
> charged with desire that it is hard to come
> to simple rest. Desire is always stronger
> than satisfaction.
>
> Put more simply, there is within us a fun-
> damental dis-ease, and unquenchable fire
> that renders us incapable, in this life, of
> ever coming to full peace.[154]

Television commercials and "half-time shows" at sporting events illustrate this with particular force. In fifteen to thirty second bursts, scantily-clad human bodies, in enticing sexual motions, vibrate to fiery blasts, exploding rockets and darting lights to "entertain" or to sell cars, beverages and relentless pleasure in a hellish glare that never ceases to writhe with the promise of satiety. How would Dante have described this graphic exploitation of human desire?

---

[154] Ronald Rolheiser, *The Holy Longing: The Search for a Christian Spirituality* (New York: Doubleday, 1999), p. 3.

Paradoxically, two different goals draw some to heroic discipline: the relentless urge for worldly success, and the religiously motivated desire for union with God. A skilled quarterback placing a spiral pass into the arms of his receiver sixty yards away knows it, and is willing to undergo merciless training to achieve it. A Maximilian Kolbe offering in Christ-love to enter a starvation pit in place of a fellow-prisoner knew it. Skateboarder and record-breaker Danny Way said it well:

> My motivation is organic its (sic) comes from deep within, my drive isn't for money and its (sic) not for fame, its (sic) not for anything but satisfying my own internal conflicts. The day I set the new record I had an issue with my getting enough speed so the following week I added more roll to the ramp to go bigger not feeling content with my accomplishment at 25.5 ft. Unfortunately on my return visit I broke my ankle so I have been hurt dwelling on this since, the ramp is still awaiting my return and this voice is (sic) my head is going to drive me insane until I'm physically ready for a rematch.[155]

---

[155] See GrindTV, Danny Way quotation with Instagram, in "Danny Way catches the biggest air on a skateboard, sets World

The drive to surpass present barriers is at once a marvelous gift and a field ripe for the temptation to be satiated by that which cannot fulfill the deepest restlessness of the heart. Each moment of human life is a call to exceed where we are and have been. Personal evil knows how to persuade the most ardent of humans to pursue fulfillment within the confines of earthly existence, as splendid as many of them can be. Jesus Christ endured these temptations and revealed them for our benefit. Turn stones into bread, said the evil one, attempting to tarnish in advance the night when the ultimate self-gift of the Lord would be expressed through bread and wine in an upper room on Jerusalem. Leap from the Temple pinnacle, the evil one further prompted. No other can survive such a dare, said the evil one (not knowing the sacred feet would step on surging seawater and survive). Get down on your knees and adore me said the spiritual self-idol, seemingly oblivious to the reality that the One he addressed was his maker.

From the Garden of Eden to Olympic Parks and genetic laboratories, illusions persist that someday humanity will realize total fulfillment apart from the divine love for which it is made. Years ago, a cartoonist captured this well. In the sketch, one hand puppet is saying to another hand puppet: "Sometimes, I wonder if there *is* a hand."

Record," http://www.grindtv.com/skateboarding/danny-way-catches-the-highest-air-on-a-skateboard-sets-world-record##GjWcsW4C9ROz01.97 (accessed Apr 5, 2016).

Boundaries are priceless gifts. There would be no angelfood cake without the sturdy funnel rising in the center of a pan and steep sides holding the fragile mix of sweet batter as it rises and bakes within an oven. There would be no tennis game without established lines and a net set at standard height. No space capsule would rise from the launching pad without intricate, interlacing systems prepared with utmost care to respect the forces of gravity, thrust and speed.

Astronauts know this acutely. The farther one desires to travel into space, the more urgent the need to be "in touch with Houston," and other brilliant scientists and technicians who monitor the intricacies of space travel. As seen in earlier chapters, creation, and in particular the earth, has a unity of composition, gravitational force, and speed of motion attuned with such perfection, that if there were even a slight deviation from the minute interaction among them all, the earth would become chaotic and would no longer sustain life as we know it. In traversing to these limits in the name of progress, the greatest care must be taken.

Above all, that applies to the limits of what it means to be a human being. To submit to limitation in order to attain greater perfection requires patient restlessness. It is a restlessness rooted in love. As noted earlier, this has to do with small beings as fragile as butterflies as well as to man-made machines hurtling into space.

SUFFERING

The inability to control what impedes, debilitates or threatens causes suffering. Attempting to fixate a moment of exquisite beauty or expression of love is impossible and is its own form of suffering. St. Augustine *prayed* his struggle to understand the meaning of time, the profoundly elusive meaning of past, present and future, in relation to the eternal "now" of God.

> See how the present time, which alone we found worthy to be called long, is contracted to hardly the space of a single day. But let us examine it also, because not even a single day is present in its totality. It is completed in twenty-four hours of night and day, and of these the first has the others still to come, the last has them past it..... If any point of time is conceived that can no longer be divided into even the most minute parts of a moment, that alone it is which can be called the present. It flies with such speed from the future into the past that it cannot be extended by even a trifling amount.[156]

---

[156] Saint Augustine, *The Confessions of St. Augustine*, trans. John K. Ryan (Garden City, New York: Doubleday, 1960), 289.

Waiting for the diagnosis of severe pain in a beloved's body, or word of a loved one's survival after a violent accident underscores Augustine's commentary on the lived *present* which "has no space," but divides before and after, and is the still-point of every "now." Hoarfrost, a passing breeze, the smallest sliver of the sun emerging over a mountain – none can be held fast or stored. It is an illusion to attempt perpetuating the "now" of a spoken wedding vow, or the feeling of the bishop's hands imposed on one's head in ordination. Each partial fulfillment of love's journey presses onward to the next. To block the "now" from impulsion forward is to bring about a chosen "still-born."

In the relationship among earthly time and waiting there is an eternal purpose. Augustine struggled with the human tendency to speak of a "long time," and a "short time" when there was simply the immeasurable "now" that separates what is past and irretrievable and the future which does not yet exist. "Time" measures a restlessness in creation that cannot be stopped. In human experience, it is like an ungraspable rope of water flowing through one's hands.

The Word of God speaks of the "Hour" for great happenings, of patient waiting, and of fulfillment of "times." John's Gospel in particular notes that in the ceaseless flow of time, there are definite moments chosen by the Father that mark turning points in the history of the universe. Jesus was keenly aware of them in his earthly journey, and even as a youth, John was sensitive to them. The future apostle would remember and write (perhaps sixty or seventy years later) that it was "about the tenth hour" when he and his unnamed companion responded to Jesus' invitation to "Come and see" (Jn 1:39) where He was staying.

The culture of Jesus' time predated clocks as we know them. Sunrise and sunset remained rather constant in the Mediterranean latitudes. A "day" was divided approximately into "twelve hours," beginning with the first hour between 6-7, the third hour at 9, the sixth at noon, and the ninth at 3 in the afternoon. When John speaks of Jesus' invitation to "Come and see" as happening at the "tenth hour," it would have meant four o'clock in the afternoon in later reckoning. When John writes of Jesus indicating His "Hour" however, the Lord was referring to the time designated by His Father for the most significant event of all history: His personal Redemption of humanity, extended to persons both before and after it was accomplished. He knew that Hour and humanly grappled with its arrival and fulfillment. From intense memory, John recalls Jesus' speaking of His "Hour." It was on "the third day" of John the Baptist's public recognition of Jesus as the Lamb of God that Jesus attended a wedding in Cana. Prompted by His Mother to perform a work of mercy for the bride and groom, Jesus tells Her "My hour has not yet come." (Jn 2:4)

Two chapters later, John says that it was "about the sixth hour" when Jesus spoke with the Samaritan woman at the well near Sychar. In clarifying the kind of water for which the woman truly thirsted, Jesus told her: "But the hour is coming, and now is, when the true worshippers will worship the Father in spirit and truth, for such the Father seeks to worship him." (Jn 4:23) The enemies of Jesus were restrained from hurling Him over the brow of a hill in Nazareth after He had made known Who He is, and how He fulfills promised hopes. To the Jews who contested His healing of a man, ill for thirty-eight years, because He had done this merciful act on the Sabbath, Jesus again spoke of time authoritatively: "Truly, truly, I say to you, the hour is coming, and now is, when the dead will hear the voice of the Son of God, and those who hear will live." (Jn 5:25) In fact, he added, "Do not marvel at this; for the hour is coming when all who are in the tombs will hear his voice and come forth, those who have done what is good, to the resurrection of life, and those who have done evil, to the resurrection of judgment." (Jn 5:28-29) Then-Pope John Paul II addressed the meaning of Jesus' Hour in a General Audience in 1998, explaining that Jesus used the word "hour" to mean the moment that His Father had determined for fulfilling the work of salvation:

> The great hour in world history occurs when the Son gives his life, making his saving voice heard to those who are under the power of sin. It is the hour of Redemption.

All of Jesus' life is directed to this hour. At an agonizing moment shortly before his passion, Jesus says: 'Now is my soul troubled. And what shall I say? "Father, save me from this hour?" No, for this purpose I have come to this hour.'(Jn 12:27)

This decisive hour is both the hour of passion and the *hour of glorification*.....'When Jesus knew that his hour had come to depart out of this world to the Father, having loved his own who were in the world, he loved them to the end' (Jn 13:1)..... The supreme hour is ultimately the moment when the Son returns to the Father.[157]

Jesus knew what it means to wait, to be obediently at-one with the Father in all of life's moments, but particularly in the "hour" of His total, salvific self-gift, subjected to the most ignominious mauling that his enemies could contrive. As Son of God, He did not attempt to control the dissolute flailing of His body in the Passion. He received it so that every sinner, regardless of the depths

---

[157] Pope John Paul II, General Audience Address, the Vatican, Jan.14, 1998, 2, 3, and 5, as translated in catholicculture.org, https://www.catholicculture.org/culture/library/view.cfm?recnum=1304 (accessed Apr.7, 2016).

of degradation reached, could ask with the dying thief of Good Friday, "Jesus, remember me when you come in your kingly power." (Lk 23:42)

How long it would have taken for reports of Jesus' "Hour" of crucifixion and resurrection to reach even the Romanized cultures surrounding the Mediterranean! The meaning of the Paschal Mystery still remains unknown to many, as Pope Francis reiterates in his call that Jesus' merciful self-gift be made known "at the peripheries" of the human family. Despite the cacophonous and instantaneous broadcasting of events and information worldwide, the deepest meaning of waiting, of suffering, and of human destiny in eternal life remains unknown or rejected among many peoples. What is a mystery is often further obscured by attempts to do away with suffering itself through pharmaceutical, technical, and self-destructive means.

Stanislaw Grygiel, in his commentary on the meaning of suffering in a secularized world, first states that suffering is more than pain in the usual meaning of the word. Pain sounds a warning, he says, announcing a malady that threatens one's life. The meaning of pain, however, cannot be reduced to revealing illness, says Grygiel. Even if we alleviate it, or completely do away with it and its causes, "the feeling of being in danger, awakened by the experience of pain, will remain in our consciousness as a part of the real condition of our being; it will speak about its truth."[158] The truth provoked by this kind of pain forecasts future afflictions and untimely death. It "resides in the core of his being and cannot be eliminated while he lives, unless he decides to commit suicide. For man himself is this pain"[159]

Whether one calls it the worm of worry or anxiety, the unsettledness caused by pain is real and nags, distracts. A major component of our suffering is the inability to choose how and when it will occur, how long it may deepen and endure – whether it will be alleviated or lead to a final passing from this life. The stubborn desire to be in control imposes itself repeatedly. Control is the capacity to influence and determine events and the practical aspects of our own and others' lives.

Christ did not deny or attempt to do away with apprehension concerning future suffering. He integrated it within the reality of love and personal self-gift. Ultimately, by taking up His cross He bore the accumulated weight of suffering unto death in His body-person. Counselor and student of literature Helen M. Luke reflected on suffering from the perspective of aging. She distinguished between two experiences of suffering – one considering it totally unproductive and depressing, the other seeing

---

[158] Stansilaw Grygiel, "The meaning of suffering in the secularized world," *Revue Theologique de Lugano* 1 (1996), in *Communio* 29 (Winter, 2002), 45.

[159] "The meaning of suffering in the secularized world," 45.

suffering as an essential condition for the "individuation" of person described by C. G. Jung. Toward the end of her work on *Old* Age, after considering works of literature from the *Odyssey* to the poetry of D. H. Lawrence and T. S. Eliot, Luke reflected in the final chapter on the meaning of suffering.

Noting that the word "suffering" is used to express varied kinds of experience, Luke turned to the Latin roots of the word: *sub* (under) and *ferre* (to bear). She said that they were reminiscent of the term "undercarriage," or "that which bears the weight of a vehicle above the wheels."[160] She found this an apt image for the meaning of human suffering. Other words to describe it, such as *affliction, grief,* and *depression* depict images of suffering as a bearing down under a weight. "Afflicted" comes from *fligere* which means to strike, and "depression" means to be pressed down, but "Only when we suffer in the full sense of the word do we *carry* the weight."[161]

It is not possible here to cite adequately how the counselor Helen Luke distinguishes between various reasons for non-acceptance of suffering in a culture where "we are all open in the unconscious to the present collective worship of grades" in every department of life, of seeking prestige and assuming a false guilt about our physical

---

[160] Helen M. Luke, *Old Age*, intro Barbara A. Mowat (New York: Parabola Books, 1987), 103.

[161] Luke, *Old Age*, 103.

and emotional weaknesses that hamper our willingness to accept suffering. It is ordinary common sense to seek appropriate help for dealing with the varieties of suffering that beset us all. It is Luke's reversal of the familiar approach to suffering as that which *presses down upon us* that speaks into an age of restlessness with particular meaning. She does not suggest a halting on the way, but a progression that accords with the Christ-experience of bearing up beneath what we are asked to suffer:

> The four-wheeled chariot is an ancient symbol of the Incarnation, and the thought of suffering as the undercarriage fits perfectly into this image. Suffering is that which carries the weight of the vehicle, distributing it over the fourfold wheels so that the driver may stand in safety and move toward the chosen goal.[162]

The image of the undercarriage as a hidden strength, sustained not by sheer determination, but love guided by divine grace, is the terrain of the saints, not in their heroic appearance, but their humble realization that the Holy Spirit is both the driver and the One who provides the wheels on which the undercarriage sustains suffering.

---

[162] *Old Age,* 107.

Just as the One who journeyed to Calvary opened the possibility of bearing all suffering with meaning, holy women and men carry the weight of suffering joined with Christ. In First Peter, the Apostle urges:

> But if when you do right and suffer for it you take it patiently, you have God's approval. For to this you have been called, because Christ also suffered for you, leaving you an example that you should follow in his steps. He committed no sin; no guile was found on his lips. When he was reviled, he did not revile in return; when he suffered he did not threaten; but he trusted him who judges justly. (I Pet 2:20-23)

Christ did not disdain fear, but in His perfect love, He bore up under all that was asked because of love. When we see elements of this lived among us, we may not even know how to name it well, but we recognize it and esteem those who outrun our own capacities of suffering out of love.

My father was such a man. One of the deepest memories of my early childhood was is willingness to lay down his life to protect my mother, my siblings and me in a mammoth Minnesota blizzard. On an early morning in February, Dad left for a three-mile journey to town to keep his appointed schedule as a mailman. During the day, severe wind developed, driving a blinding snow into steep drifts. By workday's close there was no possibility of his return to the simple small home where Mother and three of us children would spend the night. There was no running water or electricity in the house; heat came from a potbelly stove at one end of the living room. Thin glass panes rattled in the windows and bitter cold made it essential that we stay close to the stove. Mother put in small amounts of corn cobs and small pieces of wood to sustain a meagre fire, fearful that the fragile pipes fastened near the ceiling would fall when wind gusts buffeted the house. She wrapped us in featherbeds near the stove through the night. Pails of water that my brother had managed to bring from the well froze not far from the stove.

Mother kept a straightforward family diary for over forty years. There is a gap in her diary from February 9 to 13 of 1936, but she wrote of that blizzard a few days later:

> 38 [degrees] below – wind 80 mi..... We had a terrible night. The wind shook all the windows, shook the house and came in waves like an angry sea. I couldn't keep hardly any fire as there was danger of fire. Everything was freezing up. You could hear such hard lashes every now and then how things

were freezing. I was not well but kept up the fire all night.

The storm still raged the next morning. In town, against the advice of relatives with whom he had spent the night, Dad prepared to walk into the blinding blizzard, papers stuffed across his chest beneath his overcoat and a blanket wrapped about his upper body. I am told that (unlikely in that day) he asked to receive Communion, and set out. He told relatives that he would try to reached the first farmhouse on the way. If he made the first, he would go on to the second, third, and so on. He walked, following fence posts deep in snow. About eleven o'clock in the morning, my nine-year-old sister saw my Dad emerging near the house from the world of whiteness. When he came into the house, my Mother tried to "wait on him," but soon collapsed. Dad sat at her bedside, keeping watch. She suffered a heart attack, but survived it.

Suffering borne of love is measureless. In ways that were not foreseen in the latter twentieth century, the persecution of Christians in the Third Millennium has come with a new fury. Martyrdom is happening in nations as disparate as Syria, the Sudan, Yemen and Nigeria. Who can forget television images of men kneeling on the Mediterranean seacoast, knowing that within minutes they would undergo beheading – or the account of women religious, Missionaries of Charity, snatched from their convent in Yemen, tied to trees, shot, and their heads crushed. Personal evil is having its "hour" of dehumanized brutality.

Who could count the members of the human family who have known a new diaspora because of their faith and their need to flee homelands in order to protect children from these terrors? Created as pilgrims, the human family is finding that its inherent restlessness is being forced into new patterns. As in the early centuries of the Church, witnesses are suffering for the benefit of all.

MERIAM IBRAHIM

A twenty-seven year old physician, Meriam Ibrahim, was accused of adultery and apostasy under the rule of Sudan's President Omar al-Bashir who had imposed Islamic law on the country. Although a Christian her entire life, Meriam was given a death sentence for marrying Daniel Wani, a Sudanese Christian man who suffers from muscular dystrophy. Under Sharia law, Meriam was accused of "adultery" and sentenced to be punished with 100 lashes. For her so-called "apostasy" from Islam she was sentenced to be hung. Meriam and her husband had a 20 month-old son. Both sentences were to be carried out when she gave birth to the child in her womb. During her pregnancy she was held captive in a filthy prison cell with her small son. Daily she was visited in her cell by men trying to persuade her to relent, and who promised protection for her and her family if she would renounce Christianity. Meriam told her husband: "I refuse to change. I am not giving up Christianity just so that I can live. If they want to execute me then they should go ahead and do it because I'm not going to change my faith."[163]

The international community heard of the situation and clamored for Meriam's release. While in chains, Meriam gave birth to a girl, Maya, on the floor of the filthy cell, with her little boy next to her. Pressure from world leaders and celebrities prevented the Sudanese government from administering both the lashing and hanging of Meriam. Both sentences had been postponed until her child would be born. Her husband Daniel Wani, who supported her in suffering these terrors, said that he was told that his marriage to Meriam was void and the children were not his.

Following Meriam's release after international pressure, even as the young family was to leave from a Sudanese airport, they were taken captive again and subjected to interrogation. Daniel Wani said that the family

---

[163] Mark Nicol for *The Mail on Sunday* and Kieran Corcoran, "Sudanese woman facing 'barbaric' death sentence for marrying a Christian will be FREED...but her lawyer says 'I'll believe it when I see it,'" http://www.dailymail.co.uk/news/article-2644796/Sudanese-woman-facing-barbaric-death-sentence-marrying-Christian-FREED-U-turn-authorities.html (accessed Apr. 8, 2016).

was handled violently, and their defense lawyers beaten and expelled from the airport.

It is once again an age of martyrs. Interior restlessness merges with exterior waiting "for what we know not." Pope Francis in a homily for the Feast of St. Augustine noted that the saint's use of the term "restlessness" was striking. It led him to reflect on three areas that should make every Christian restless: the search for God, the desire to share the Gospel, and their love for everyone they meet.[164]

> Augustine lived a life like that of many young people today, the pope said..... He studied, he had fun, 'he knew intense love' and began a brilliant career as a teacher of rhetoric, the pope said. 'He had arrived in every way'..... But in his heart, there remained the restlessness of the search for the profound meaning of life,' Pope Francis said. 'His heart was not asleep, it was not anesthetized by success, by things, by power.... 'he discovered that God was waiting for him and, in fact, never stopped looking for him

---

[164] See Pope Francis, "Pope says Christians should have restless hearts like St. Augustine's," http://ncronline.org/news/vatican/pope-says-christians-should-have-restless-hearts-st-augustines (accessed Apr. 8, 2016).

first..... look into your hearts and ask yourself if you have a heart that wants great things or a heart that is asleep. Has your heart maintained that restlessness or has it been suffocated by things?'[165]

---

[165] Pope Francis, "Pope says Christians should have restless hearts."

Chapter VI

VIBRANT INTERCHANGE: THE COMMUNION OF SAINTS

The immediate stuff of the prayer life of the Christian people in its corporate anxiety and hope is perhaps best grasped in the Litany of the Saints..... this litany grew up by degrees from the Late Antique period onwards. It absorbed into itself all those concerns with which time harries us, while counterposing to them the pledge of hope through whose agency we may endure them..... the walls separating heaven and earth, and past, present and future, are now as glass. The Christian lives in the presence of the saints as his own proper ambience, and so lives 'eschatologically.'[166]

---

[166] Joseph Ratzinger, *Eschatology: Death and Eternal Life*, 2nd ed, trans Michael Waldstein, trans ed Aidan Nichols (Washington DC: The

hy is there fear of dying? What does it mean that heaven is eternal life with God – of seeing God face to face? Who *is* God? These are questions, spoken and sometimes only fearfully thought, that underlie so much of restlessness in the human heart. Having opened so many other questions in earlier chapters of this book, it is essential to focus on ultimate questions that keep nagging beneath lesser, sometimes more mundane ones.

Why is dying fearful? The unknown is unsettling and fear arises quickly, for example, regarding matters of one's health. A pain can scurry up the inner wall of skin and thought, needling us, asking from within: how serious is this? One's own "interior friend of Job" may suggest that "something dreadful has latched on to you from which you will never arise." A new pain or feeling of bodily helplessness occurs: could this be the beginning of a serious disease that will debilitate, bring great suffering? Or could it actually be the beginning of my dying? We are body-persons and every pain, or inability to carry out a familiar activity is a reminder of the fragility of human life, a reminder of death, even if we do not *consciously* advert to that as we staunch a wound or take an antibiotic. It is never just an organ of the body or a finger that is ill or suffering: it is the whole person.

Catholic Univ. of America Press, 1988), 8-9.

Even as new remedies for specific health problems are offered that were unknown in the past, new fears are raised. Omni-present advertisements for medical products often give a two-edged message. On the one hand, sufferers will be urged to buy a product while viewing images of healthy adults happily playing a round of golf or having an outing with exuberant grandchildren. On the other hand, these images are accompanied by swiftly-spoken and insurance-guarded messages listing all the possible adverse side-effects that may result from the product's use – from nausea and kidney failure to a heart attack, stroke, or possible death.

There is indeed a new intensity in remembering Christ's warning to be alert, ready, because we "do not know the day nor the hour" when our precious life on this earth will end. Countries that formerly seemed to have stable governments and means of civilian protection are no longer able to assure safety for their citizens. Children are warned to be on guard against abusive actions which threaten them from within their families, schools, sports programs and churches. There are different reasons for the increase in these dangers, including the breakdown of marriage and family life and entire cultures' losses of shared moral principles. Danger now lurks where safety was once presumed, and sudden death from acts of violence and terror have become commonplace.

Repeatedly, Jesus said, "Do not be afraid." Whether it was to the ruler of the synagogue whose child was dying, or the Apostles fearful of death by storm on the Sea of Galilee – or their seeing Him walk toward them on the swirling waters of the Sea of Galilee at night. Jesus spoke into their fear of death with an assuring "Do not be afraid." Keith Fournier writes that "All of our fears find a common root in the fear of death which can lead to the living slavery spoken of in the Letter to the Hebrews..... 'Now since the children share in blood and flesh, he likewise shared in them, that through death he might destroy the one who has the power of death, that is, the devil, and free those who through fear of death had been subject to slavery all their life.' (Heb 2:14-15)"[167]

Death is the only reality common to every living person on earth. Although we can escape many disasters and diseases over a long life, each of us will die. It is that realization that Fournier names when he says that "All of our fears find a common root in the fear of death." In Gethsemane, Christ knew the horrors that awaited Him the following day and allowed that realization to penetrate His sacred body. Luke's Gospel says: "And being in an agony he prayed more earnestly; and his sweat became like great drops of blood falling down upon the ground." (Lk 22:44)

---

[167] Keith Fournier, "Fear is Useless," *Catholic Online*, http://www.catholic.org/featured/headline.php?ID=2592 (accessed Apr. 11, 2016).

Over a lifetime, how often have we been close to death, and perhaps not even been aware of it? It is amazing that anyone "grows up" and then attains adulthood and advanced age after having countless encounters with lesser forms of death. How varied, also, the age at which the first intimations of death come to a child. I recall a young grandfather relating an incident about his two-year-old granddaughter. She stepped on a caterpillar on the sidewalk, he said, and then looked down at it and said softly: "No more." Children who play violent games on hand-held electronic devices learn how to be skillful and rapid at eliminating characters in those games. Then they watch television's violent news reports and dramas. Since they are so familiar with images of death, virtual and actual, they may not be able to distinguish the finality of genuine death in the way that the two-year-old girl who stepped on a caterpillar intuitively *knew* it.

Some years ago it was reported that a girl in Japan, in a lower grade of an elementary school, brutally murdered another girl in the school's washroom. The next day, when the perpetrator was brought before authorities and questioned about it, the girl asked that the one she had murdered be brought there so that she could apologize. From playing games in which "enemies" could be killed day after day (and then electronically revived the next day) she was confused in distinguishing between real, permanent death and contrived virtual death.

To survive extreme danger and out-maneuver what seems sure death – these are themes that fascinate adults as well as children. Super-human, trans-human activities and new forms of weaponry are featured in films and novels. Heroes and heroines "outsmart" evil enemies bent on bringing about death. Their *activity* in countering death both sates desire for great skill and speed and whets the appetite for speedier (and often more exotic) weapons and maneuvers.

Paul Wong asks why, on the one hand, so few people have found acceptance of death. "The answer, I believe," he says, "lies in our Western Society; we live in a death-denying culture. We want to delay and slow the dying process through medical science, diet, and exercise. We want to maintain the illusion of youth through plastic surgery and adopting an active life style."[168]

On the other hand, there is a more extreme form of death denial, says Wong. It is the Life Extension Movement, which declares *death* a mortal disaster, a holocaust killing fifty million people a year. He says that the Movement is waging war against death on several fronts: first, there are "calorie minimizers" who eat as little food as possible. This lowers their body temperature and slows down their metabolism, but they "are a walking death – pale, cold

---

[168] Paul T. P. Wong, "A Meaning Management Model," Trinity Western University, BC, Canada, http://www.meaning.ca/archives/archive/art_death-acceptance_P_Wong.htm. (accessed Apr. 11, 2016).

and lacking vitality. They want to prolong their existence at the expense of the joy of living."[169] The Life Extension Movement also includes "the supplementarians," who are obsessed with physical health and use vitamin pills and Chinese herbs to slow down the process of aging; and Third, are "the cryonicists" who pay extravagant amounts of money to have their head, or total body frozen in liquid nitrogen "until science finds a way to resurrect them." [170] Wong points out that while all organisms die, only humans have the cognitive capacity to be aware of it, and to fear what follows.

Death, apart from faith in the Living Christ, can become a matter for personal decision and control. Suicide, assisted suicide, and "right to die" movements have become commonplace. The United States' National Center for Injury Prevention and Control reported that "Suicide was the tenth leading cause of death for all ages in 2013."[171] In the same year, the report showed that 17% of United States students in grades 9-12 had seriously considered attempting to commit suicide in the previous year. Four states permit PAS (Physician Assisted Suicide) and by 2015, eighteen more states and the District of Columbia

---

[169] Wong, "A Meaning Management Model."

[170] Wong, "A Meaning Management Model."

[171] "Suicide," National Center for Injury Prevention and Control, www. cdc.gov/violenceprevention (accessed Apr. 12, 2016).

were considering whether to allow it.[172] Ryan Anderson names (from a reasoned human stance) four problems that show why legalization of physician-assisted suicide is a grave mistake: it endangers the weak and vulnerable; it corrupts the practice of medicine and the doctor-patient relationship; it compromises the family and intergenerational commitments; and it betrays human dignity and equality before the law.[173]

Krista Kafer, who assisted her father as he suffered from terminal cancer, is a hospice volunteer and says "I know how brutal dying can be. The fear of helplessness or suffering and the desire to end a person's suffering is only human," she writes, but enabling suicide is not the answer:

> What begins as a legal framework for doctor-assisted suicide for consenting terminally adult patients ends in a far darker place. In addition to the thousands of Dutch and Belgian adults who choose to commit suicide each year with doctor support an untold number of disabled newborns, sick children, comatose patients, and patients

---

[172] Ryan T. Anderson, "Four Problems with Physician-Assisted Suicide, http://www.heritage.org/research/reports/2015/03/four-problems-with-physi (accessed Apr. 12, 2016).

[173] Anderson, "Four Problems with Physician-Assisted Suicide."

with dementia are killed without their consent.[174]

After prisoners in concentration camps were liberated in the concluding days of World War II, there was general horror over genocide, and the experiments performed on human bodies when the Nazis attempted to re-make humanity in their own image. Currently, many "good" people have become so accustomed to available ways of ending life that the idea no longer evokes a moral sense of revulsion. Abortion, the selling of dismembered bodies taken from the womb, and the hastened deaths of the helpless aged are all relativized under a protocol of respecting individual choice, or a so-called "common good."

An amaze-less familiarity with violent death in its many forms, and the ready *disposal* of what proves difficult can assail the union of faith and reason in approaching the mysteries of life and death. A holy and genuine restlessness in the face of death can now be assuaged by what one commentator described as a "wink and nod" understanding among some medical professionals who stretch restraints of statutes surrounding legalized assisted suicide.

---

[174] Krista Kafer, "How Assisted Suicide Becomes a License to Kill," http://thefederalist.com/2016/02/16/how-assisted-suicide-becomes-a-license (accessed Apr. 12, 2016).

Fear of the unknown and the experience (or expectation) of excruciating pain, together with a desire to control one's own destiny can combine to tempt a person to draw the curtain of life and ask for what seems a final solution to the problem of life's restlessness. St. Paul wrote to members of the young church in Corinth:

> Do you not know that your body is a temple of the Holy Spirit within you, which you have from God? You are not your own; you were bought with a price. So glorify God in your body..... No temptation has overtaken you that is not common to man. God is faithful, and he will not let you be tempted beyond your strength, but with the temptation will also provide the way of escape, that you may be able to endure it. (I Cor 6:19-20; 10:13)

I recall hearing that the pressure upon the body of a child passing through the birth canal of its mother is so great that the body could not survive a comparable pressure in another stage of life. It is a blessing that the enwombed child does not know what will be required to go through that passage, or it might refuse.

Imagine for a moment that the fetus *could* reason. Curled in a fetal position, the unborn one is held in place by warm walls of the maternal body. All of its needs for survival are being met. Imagine the mother saying to her child: in a little while you are going to leave this womb. Hands will grapple with your body; you will feel cool air and gasp for a first breath. There will be bright lights around you and you will be cleansed and wrapped not in flesh but cloth, cry for food and sleep in a little crib. That's not all! Before long you will see faces and colors and hear your name called again and again. Soon you will crawl, then stand and run. But first, you must leave here and pass through a dark tunnel and it will cause you pain. No matter how much the mother would explain in detail what lay ahead, and no matter how much the child's IQ will measure someday, there would be no way that the child of nine months, curled in upon herself would be able to comprehend what it will mean to breathe, to see and eat, to laugh and run. *She will need to make the passage first,* or be carefully lifted from the womb into glaring light with a sudden need to breathe.

It would not be a kindness but a travesty to convince the enwombed child that it wasn't worth the journey through the birth canal, or that no one could expect her to be equal to the difficult task of submitting to the rigors and adventure of coming into the larger world. It would not be loving to convince the unborn fetus that it would be better to have things stop where they were – that it was just an illusion that a wonderful world and incredible relationships awaited their emergence from the womb.

Little one, you can decide right now that you don't need or want to go through all that. You can be stillborn and not even feel it. Yet, analogically, that is being told to persons of all ages who are undergoing some manner of suffering – chosen death intended as a humane "kindness" instead of natural death chosen by a loving God at an "hour" not of their choosing.

Analogically, no matter how much has been said of the significance of death and the splendor of eternal life, we will only know and experience it after the passage through death — whether it be through a painful dark tunnel, or whether we will be lifted from this present life quickly (like a child in Caesarian birth) through a heart attack or an accident. There is a tremendous dignity in the often awkward, helpless, needy aspects of dying. Barbara Karnes, RN, writes in "Terminal Restlessness":

> Terminal restlessness is a medical term for the restlessness and agitation that often begins one to three weeks before death from disease.

> The restlessness shows itself by random body movements, hands picking the air or clothing, by just not being settled or quiet.

This restlessness can be a lack of oxygen
to the brain but more likely it is just fear
showing itself. The body is expressing what
it is feeling because the person is beyond
expressing with words..... We are all going
to be afraid to some degree as we approach
death. This is normal and natural. Also we
know when we are dying. It is no secret. We
live inside of our bodies – we know..... The
restlessness is just part of the way we die.[175]

Each person's death is unique. Each person's restlessness regarding death is also unique, and can even fore-
shadow martyrdom in an extraordinary way, as witnessed
by Father Christian-Marie de Cherge, one of seven French
Trappist monks slain in Algeria in May of 1996. Although
there is ambiguity regarding direct responsibility for the
brutal slaying of these monks, Father de Cherge foresaw
it. Somewhere between December 1, 1993 and January 1,
1994, he sent a letter to his family in France. It was marked
to be opened at his death. It was a letter written in the spirit
of early Christian martyrs such as St. Stephen, St. Paul, St.
Polycarp, and St. Ignatius of Antioch. The Trappist wrote
at a time when terrorism was engulfing foreigners living

---

[175] Barbara Barnes, "Terminal Restlessness," Oct.1, 2012, End of
life education materials for families and professionals, TAGS
Approaching Death (/taxonomy/term/38), (accessed May 11, 2016).

in Algeria. Father de Cherge said that he wanted his family, community and Church to remember that his life was given to God and to "this country." He asked that his family pray for him that he would have the lucidity to beg God's pardon "and that of all my fellow human beings, while pardoning with all my heart anyone who might have hurt me":

> I could never wish such a death. It seems important to profess that.

> In fact, I do not see how I could rejoice that these people that I love should be indiscriminately blamed for my murder.

> If the price of the grace of martyrdom is that one has to die at the hand of an Algerian, whoever he may be, then it is too high – especially if he professes to be acting in accord with what he believes is Islam.....

> For life lost, totally mine and totally theirs, I give thanks to God, who seems to have wanted it to be utterly so, for this joy, through and despite everything.....

> And you, too, my last-minute friend, you who know not what you do.

Yes, for you too I wish this thank you, and
this adieu which is of your planning.

May we meet each other again, happy
thieves, in paradise, should it please God,
the Father of us. Amen![176]

From the fateful choice of woman and man at the
beginning of human existence, suffering is intrinsically
part of human life and will have a profound influence on
the meaning of eternal life for every person. Ladislaus
Boros underscores Jesus' parable of the Last Judgment
which is "not symbolic language. It must be understood
in all its hard truth. It is true that spiritual need, inner
imprisonment and hunger of soul, are also hard realities."[177] Boros noted that it is the *most* terrible experience
for a person to say "I have nobody." Yet, response in love
to such a person is the condition for entering heaven. It is
not ecstasy in prayer or having a thorough knowledge of
laws and prescriptions that makes one Christian, but how
one has shown selfless service to the abandoned in daily
life – those who are saying "I have nobody."

---

[176] Father Christian-Marie de Cherge, "Letter from martyred monk,"
first published by *La Croix*, French daily Catholic newspaper, May
29, and in English trans. in *Origins*, June 13, 1996.

[177] Ladislaus Boros, "Suffering and Death: Question and Answer," *The
Way*, Vol. 7, No.1, Winter, 1967, 52.

In recent times, many persons have described "near-death experiences" which have radically changed their fears about dying. Some accounts have elements in common, such as being able to "look down" upon those attending to their bodies and to remember what they saw. Often these descriptions also include the experience of passing through a dark tunnel and seeing a brilliant light approaching. The light is experienced as personal, non-threatening, but questioning them about satisfaction with their life (which flashes totally before them, chronologically, in an instant). Often there is a sense of peace and beauty, together with a desire to proceed and not return to their earthly body. These are not "measurable" experiences that can be monitored technically nor interpreted scientifically. The accounts are not identical, but some are rather similar. In his book *Life After Life: The Investigation of a Phenomenon – Survival of Bodily Death*, Raymond A. Moody quotes from a number of persons whose near-death experiences were shared with him. Moody writes:

> There is a remarkable agreement in the 'lessons,' as it were, which have been brought back from these close encounters with death. Almost everyone has stressed the importance in this life of trying to cultivate love for others, a love of a unique and profound kind. One man who met the being

of life felt totally loved and accepted, even while his whole life was displayed in a panorama for the being to see.[178]

ETERNAL LIFE

Eschatology, or the study of the "four last things" of death, heaven, hell and purgatory, has been reflected upon in significant ways by theologians in the past hundred years. The First and Second World Wars, the Holocaust, the dropping of atomic bombs on Hiroshima and Nagasaki, the horrendous number of abortions, and wars in Korea, Vietnam, African nations and Near Eastern Asian lands have brought worldwide attention to the constant presence of terror and violent death. Among theologians who addressed eschatology in significant ways are Pope Emeritus Benedict XVI, Karl Rahner, and Ladislaus Boros. How understand the meaning of life after death on an earth that is steeped in death? Boros said:

> The world is pointing to heaven. The end is the true beginning. According to the original plan of creation, the world should have passed over from paradise to heaven

---

[178] Raymond A. Moody, Jr., *Life After Life: The investigation of a phenomenon – survival of bodily death* (Atlanta: Mockingbird Books, 1975), 67.

without any destruction, suffering or death. As things are now, because Christ became man and conquered death, and opened the way to heaven once more, the world moves infallibly and indubitably toward heaven.

But what is heaven? We do not know precisely..... The Easter event is not an isolated and limited fact in the history of salvation, but the sacred destiny of the whole world. Through his resurrection, Christ has spoken his effective and creative word upon the whole universe. It has already begun: 'See, I make all things new.'[179]

"But what is heaven?" asks Boros. So much of restlessness regarding eternal life is contained in that question. Although many believe in eternal life and have a desire to "get to heaven," the answer that Boros gives to his own question is significant. It echoes a certain lack of enthusiasm regarding the promise of heaven as the total fulfillment of human life – and the meaning of the universe.

I suggest that there are several reasons for this: first, as noted earlier, until we have passed from the present experience of life on earth into a new way of being with God

---

[179] "Suffering and Death: Question and Answer," 50.

in glory, we simply do not have the *capacity* to see, experience, or explain in ordinary terminology what it means to be with the Trinity in heavenly glory. *What will respond to the restlessness of the human heart?* Second, even the celebratory language of Scripture and the Church's liturgy describing heavenly glory are quite abstract, or lacking in their expression of *what can fulfill a restlessness for total fulfillment of human longing.* Third, God may seem abstract, impersonal, and lacking in vitality. It is good to ponder these, remembering as Boros says, that "we do not know precisely" what heaven is.

WHAT IS HEAVEN LIKE?

St. Paul, in his first Letter to the tough, port-smart people of the early Church in Corinth said that he was imparting to them a "secret and hidden wisdom of God, which God decreed before the ages for our glorification." (I Cor 2:7) In fact, if the rulers of that age had understood it, they would not have crucified the Lord of glory. "But, as it is written, 'What no eye has seen, nor ear heard, nor the heart of man conceived, what God has prepared for those who love him.' (I Cor. 2:9) Further on, in Chapter 15, St. Paul will caution them not to ask *how* the dead are raised, or "With what kind of body do they come? You foolish man!" (I Cor 15:35-36) Instead, he says "What you sow does not come to life unless it dies. And what you sow is not the body which is to be, but a bare kernel, perhaps of wheat or some other grain. But God gives it a body as he has chosen, and to each kind of seed its own body." (I Cor 15:36-38).

Then, in a marvelous way, St. Paul opens a window on the transformation awaiting not only humanity, but the universe:

> For not all flesh is alike, but there is one kind for men, another for animals, another for birds, and another for fish. There are celestial bodies and there are terrestrial bodies; but the glory of the celestial is one, and the glory of the terrestrial is another. There is one glory of the sun, and another glory of the moon, and another glory of the stars; for star differs from star in glory.
>
> So it is with the resurrection of the dead. What is sown is perishable, what is raised is imperishable. It is sown in dishonor, it is raised in glory..... Lo! I tell you a mystery. We shall not all sleep, but we shall all be changed..... When the perishable puts on the imperishable, and the mortal puts on immortality, then shall come to pass the saying that is written: 'Death is swallowed up in victory.' 'O death, where is thy victory?

O death, where is thy sting? (I Cor. 15:39-43; 51; 54-55)

St. Paul was writing of the meaning of death and eternal life to the people of Corinth, a city known for its temple of Aphrodite on the Acrocorinth, with its storied thousand prostitutes. One commentator says that it was easy to see why Paul would have chosen Corinth as headquarters for his mission to the West. He was not intimidated by a city that was "young, dynamic, not hidebound by tradition, a mix of dislocated individuals without strong ethnic identities"[180] who were seeking to overcome low status in a cosmopolitan hub. He would not speak to them of Christ's resurrection and their own call to eternal life in terms of even the best stultified tranquil earthly existence. Rather, in responding to the early Church in Corinth concerning their questions about the body, resurrection, and eternal life, St. Paul wrote vibrantly about what can be known in promise about the life to come.

Perhaps one reason that many believers are not "excited" about eternal life is that the imagery used for heaven seems bland or disconnected from what makes the heart restless in present life. This is echoed in humor – which often reflects real concerns of ordinary people. Many cartoons and examples from "stand-up comedy"

---

[180] "Corinth," http://www.abrock.com/Greece-Turkey/corinth.html (accessed Apr. 14, 2016).

reflect a notion that eternal life will be boring, static, an escape from hell, but lacking in meaningful activity. There are many cartoons that sketch St. Peter at heaven's entrance gate, marking off entrants with a feather quill, and having wry comments to make about prospective entrants through the "pearly gates." Peter's dowdy robe will have wings attached that cast him as an unlikely angelic figure, and he sometimes is pictured as harried and wearing a very earthy mustache. Likewise, his comments and questions are those of a man looking for foibles or obstacles to one's entry into heaven (often arising from marital foibles). Further, once granted entry, a prospective "saved person" is pictured seated on a puffy cloud, harp in hand, having innocuous conversation with another cloud-sitter. This is not, however, a reflection of saints who had earthly lives filled with a witness to love relationships with Divine Persons and heroic service unto martyrdom.

The language and imagery concerning eternal glory in the Book of Revelation can also seem far removed from contemporary experience, even though panoramic performances at the opening of Olympic Games attempt to portray in splendid precision, light, and color a kind of supra-earthly gathering that exalts human accomplishment.

Today, mass media's ceaseless bombardment of the senses in sight and sound has dulled the capacity to focus well. When heaven is described as the joyful, eternal

"Casting of golden thrones on a glassy sea," there may not be an enthusiastic response. The *reality* of heaven can easily be lost in the similes, metaphors and allegorical language used in revealing what is sacred mystery, the undeserved fulfillment of humanity.

The *Catechism of the Catholic Church* quotes the dogmatic definition of eternal life with God that Pope Benedict XII issued in 1336, in which the Pope says that "already before they take up their bodies again and before the general judgment," the souls of those purified of sin either before death or when they have been purified after death are "in heaven, in the heavenly Kingdom and celestial paradise with Christ, joined to the company of the holy angels. Since the Passion and death of Our Lord Jesus Christ, these souls have seen and do see the divine essence with an intuitive vision, and even face-to-face, without the mediation of any creature."[181] Further:

> This perfect life with the Most Holy Trinity
> – this communion of life and love with the
> Trinity, with the Virgin Mary, the angels
> and all the blessed – is called 'heaven.'
> Heaven is the ultimate end and fulfillment

---

[181] English trans *Laetamur Magnopere* in *Catechism of the Catholic Church*, 2nd ed (Citta de Vaticano: Libreria Editrice Vaticana) and (Washington, DC: USCCB, 1994), # 1023.

of the deepest human longings, the state of supreme, definitive happiness." (#1024)

To live in heaven is 'to be with Christ.' The elect live 'in Christ,' but they retain, or rather find, their true identity, their own name. (#1025)

There are only seven paragraphs in the *Catechism* devoted specifically to "heaven." What is affirmed there, however, are spare statements of the full realization of all that the restless heart has longed for during the brief time of earthly life. Heaven is not depicted as a place of endless passivity. Paragraph #1029 says that "In the glory of heaven the blessed continue joyfully to fulfill God's will *in relation to other men and to all creation.*[emphasis mine] Already they reign with Christ; with him 'they shall reign forever and ever.'" What the *Catechism* underscores is a vibrant state of being in which there is an unbreakable love-communion with the Trinity, made possible through Christ's total saving self-gift. There is an emphasis on the intimate seeing of God face-to-face, together with an ongoing relationship to others and to all creation. In heaven, we will know our true identity and how it is uniquely named.

It is certain that the restlessness of this present life and all creation will not come to a standstill in heaven, or be monotonous celebrations. Neither will heaven be heedlessly granted to everyone regardless of their choices in earthly existence.

In responding to the question, "What Will Be Our Activities in Heaven?" Jack Cottrell conjectures that since heaven is a place of rest, it may seem an absence of productive activity. While this "rest" may be the cessation of toil and mental stress, it does not mean rest from activity.[182] Cottrell assumes that there will be endless mental challenges in heaven and a new universe to probe and explore.

Experience of daily life on this earth makes it obvious that human understanding of love is flawed and often misnamed where there is lust, violence, greed, and corrupt desire to cause brutal pain and suffering. This can end in a total rejection of Divine love and a handing oneself over to evil and the powers of darkness. "To die in mortal sin without repenting and accepting God's merciful love means remaining separated from him forever by our own free choice. This state of definitive self-exclusion from God and the blessed is called 'hell.'"[183]

A person can live in ignorance, or lack of honesty, (sometimes for much of a lifetime) in abeyance of divine

---

[182] See Jack Cottrell, "What Will Be Our Activities in Heaven?" http:// jackcottrell.com/notes/what-will-be-our-activities-in-heaven/ (accessed Apr. 14, 2016).

[183] *Catechism of the Catholic Church*, #1033.

love, counting on one's prideful self-reliance. It is not surprising that when a person dies, even if they die a friend of God, there may be need for cleansing, a realization that much still needs to be purified. This is the meaning of the Mercy-gift of Purgatory. Once again, until one dies and is in that state, it is not possible to know "what it will be like." We can have intimations of the goodness of Purgatory, though. I think of watching the interview of an older woman who reflected on murders she had committed in her youth. After decades of serving prison terms and receiving professional assistance in facing the realities surrounding her crime, she now told straightforwardly what she had done in a spirit of transparent sorrow and with *gratitude* that she had become capable of the truth regarding her own person and responsibility. Listening to her testimony was helpful in understanding something of the reality of Purgatory. It is good to ask of oneself: If I were to die suddenly this day, how much would still remain to be "finished" regarding the *consequences* of my sinfulness, faults, and lack of love?

FREE WILL AND THE NECESITY OF CHOICE

Personal choice is of great concern in the "public square" today. Often it is taken to mean having the option to do whatever seems most desirable and immediate, free of intervention from legal and religious boundaries. This particularly applies in affluent societies, where multiple alternatives are available for a price. For every kind of difficulty there is a suggested, or advertised, service that will provide a "way out." A climate of moral relativism makes it seem that whatever an individual decides must be honored as having equal validity with every other choice. The question of responsibility to a transcendent creator and to fellow-humans can then seem oppressive. This position was succinctly expressed by the majority report of the Supreme Court of the United States in the case of "Planned Parenthood of Southeastern Pennsylvania, 505 U.S. 833 (1992)." An incredible portion of that report reads:

> At the heart of liberty is the right to define one's own concept of existence, of the meaning of the universe and the mystery of human life.[184]

This assertion, written into a majority report of the United States Supreme Court dismisses the basis for *any* document or statement of principles beyond those held by an individual at any given time. *It states that every individual has the "right" to define the meaning of all that exists.*

---

[184] "Planned Parenthood of Southeastern Pennsylvania vs. Casey, Governor of Pennsylvania, 505 U.S. 833 (1992)" in "American Injustice: A Way That Seems Right," http://www.fa-ir.org/ai/casey.htm (accessed Apr. 15, 2016).

There is no notion of responsibility on the part of an individual for defining these meanings, simply an assumption that each individual who has *received* life and existence in the universe may *by right* decide what it means. The absurdity of this statement (prior to any notion of the chaos it invites) helps to explain some of the turmoil now evident on the face of the earth, but it remains unchallenged in a largely secularized world community saturated by random violence and brutal means of torture and death.

A certain brashness often characterizes attitudes towards the reality of hell in our time. Even people of faith are heard to make light of it – or make statements such as "Remember when we used to think that there was a hell?" If there is a conviction that each individual determines the meaning of existence, such comments seem plausible.

Choice is a divine gift to angels and human persons. Rightly understood, it involves the ability to select between good and evil, between what is rational and what is unreasonable – even absurd. In its finality, *choice* involves eternal consequences: a human death open to eternal life with God, or to everlasting perdition. Hell is a state of being in which the restlessness of the human heart is forsaken for a frenzy never to be satisfied. The *Catechism of the Catholic Church* affirms:

We cannot be united with God unless we freely choose to love him..... To die in mortal sin without repenting and accepting God's merciful love means remaining separated from him forever by our own free choice. This state of definitive self-exclusion from God and the blessed is called 'hell.' (#1033)

The affirmations of Sacred Scripture and the teachings of the Church on the subject of hell are a *call to the responsibility* incumbent on man to make use of his freedom in view of his eternal destiny. (#1036)

The chief punishment of hell is eternal separation from God in whom alone man can possess the life and happiness for which he was created and for which he longs. (#1035)

The gift of free will and human choice concern not only small matters, but those which have eternal consequences and impart a tremendous dignity to the interior faculties of thought and will. This helps in understanding the depth of human restlessness and why the human heart will not find "rest" in limited (often perverse) imitations of divine love.

THE COMMUNION OF SAINTS

Each time that we profess the Creed, we reaffirm our belief in "The Communion of Saints." This union is sometimes described as communion among the Pilgrim Church on earth, The Church Being purified in Purgatory, and the Church in Glory. Quoting Pope Paul VI' *Credo of the People of God*, the *Catechism* avers:

> 'We believe in the communion of all the faithful of Christ, those who are pilgrims on earth, the dead who are being purified, and the blessed in heaven, all together forming one Church and we believe that in this communion, the merciful love of God and his saints is always [attentive] to our prayers' (Paul VI, *CPG* #30).[185]

The Acts of the Apostles fairly leaps with accounts of activity among the Post-Resurrection followers of Jesus and divinely-sent messengers. The Apostles experienced this in the heady days following Christ's Resurrection and the Holy Spirit's coming at Pentecost. As on Easter Day itself, there were many comings and goings, heartening surprises, and enabling gifts of the Holy Spirit – a joyful

---

[185] *Catechism*, #962.

restlessness and a being-surprised by God that was coupled with a more hesitant discernment at times.

Just prior to his Ascension, Jesus told His first followers to wait in Jerusalem until they would be "baptized by the Holy Spirit." (Acts 1:5) The Holy Spirit came on the morning of Pentecost with a sound "like of a mighty wind" that filled the whole house where they were sitting, "and there appeared to them tongues as of fire, distributed and resting on each one of them." Further, they "began to speak in other tongues." (See Acts 2:1-4)

The account of Pentecost is so familiar to us that it is difficult to know what this emphatic personal coming must have meant for fishermen who were used to watching nets through "catchless nights" and for men familiar with taxes, trading, and the simple life of small towns in Galilee. Even Mary – who had conceived by the Holy Spirit, parented the boy Jesus, and pondered His mysteries throughout his first thirty years (but had so recently suffered the Passion in its horrendous details) must have known ecstatic response to this new coming of the Holy Spirit. Suddenly, the cowering fisherman Peter was able to stand on Mount Zion and unfold the meaning of the Paschal Mystery for a large audience. He whom the Lord had looked upon intently after three denials, was enabled to do what seemed humanly impossible. In the Holy Spirit, Peter told the crippled man at the Beautiful Gate of the temple to "look" at him and John and then gave him not gold or silver, but the assured message: "In the name of Jesus Christ of Nazareth, walk." (Acts 3:6)

Signs and wonders accompanied those first days of the early Church. Peter and his companions who used to swing fish nets into the Sea of Galilee night after night now spoke fearlessly of the Risen Lord to men who were versed in the Law. Apostles were arrested and securely locked in a common prison, "But at night an angel of the Lord opened the prison doors and brought them out," telling them to go to the temple and "speak to the people all the words of this Life." (Acts 5:19-20). And they did.

An angel of the Lord told Philip to "arise," go south to the desert road leading from Jerusalem to Gaza. He did. There, the eunuch in charge of the Ethiopian queen's treasure was reading from the prophet Isaiah as he journeyed home from worshipping in Jerusalem. The Spirit told Philip "Go up and join this chariot." (Acts 8:29) He did. The Ethiopian eunuch was reading from Isaiah. Philip asked if the man understood what he was reading. "How can I, unless some one guides me?" (Acts 8:31) Philip was invited into the eunuch's chariot, and answered the man's questions with a Spirit-inspired clarity that allowed the eunuch to receive the gift of faith, desire Baptism, and receive the Sacrament on his journey home. As the eunuch proceeded rejoicing toward Ethiopia, Philip was whisked away to Azotus by the Holy Spirit (See Acts 8:39-40). There was no need for him to wait for a local caravan going north. With what ease St. Luke describes how the Spirit guided and "transported" Philip.

Peter was given a vision that clarified his perplexity about eating "unclean" foods with gentiles. Again, the Spirit directed Peter and the gentile Cornelius, his kinsmen and friends, in their communication with one another, in traveling accurately, and in resolving a divisive issue. (See Acts 10: 9-48)

How familiar, swift, yet humanly-unplanned were those interactions between heaven and earth! Estimates vary regarding the time-frame for Luke's writing of The Acts of the Apostles. Two possibilities are between 60-130 or 80-150. The Acts of the Apostles, then, are not the musings of someone far removed from the events related there. Members of the early Church who knew person-ally of events described in Acts may still have been living when the work was written, and could have contested what seemed exaggerations or made-for-effect stories.

COMMUNING WITH SAINTS AND ANGELS TODAY

Many may question the possibility of relating to family members or friends who have died, or those who have been officially named saints. Do many people speak to their guardian angels? Even as I write this, I ask the help of those who have been part of my earthly life, have died, but with whom I retain a vital relationship. It is no conundrum that close relationships in earthly life should continue when persons we have known die and are no longer inhibited by the limitations of space and time

Then-Cardinal Joseph Ratzinger pointed out the importance of the Litany of All Saints, which in addition to calling upon saint after saint on our behalf, asks their prayer for the living, specifying dangers encountered in daily life, and requesting help to grow toward all that the restless heart desires. In the liturgical celebration of the sacrament of Ordination, the men to be ordained prostrate before the altar in the presence of the Community while the Litany of the Saints is sung over them. The same liturgical rite is sung over many religious women on the day of their final profession or Consecration.

Above all, it is in the celebration of the Mass that the Communion of Saints prays together in union with Christ in His living and present self-gift. No matter what Eucharistic Canon is chosen for a Mass, there is the keen recognition of union among all three groups that come together in the unity of the Church, Christ's Body. Saints who lived throughout different centuries are recalled (some by name) and the angels are invoked to bring the offering and prayers of the earthly Church to the Heavenly Father together with Christ. The First Eucharistic Canon, for example, includes remembrances of the threefold membership in the Church interweaving the gathering at Mass of pilgrims, saints, and those in purgation:

In humble prayer we ask you, Almighty God: command that these gifts be borne by the hands of your holy Angel to your altar on high in the sight of your divine majesty, so that all of us, who through this participation at the altar receive the most holy Body and Blood of your Son, may be filled with every grace and heavenly blessing. Through Christ our Lord, Amen. Remember also, Lord, your servants N. and N., who have gone before us with the sign of faith and rest in the sleep of peace..... To us, also..... graciously grant some share and fellowship with your holy Apostles and Martyrs...[186]

In the quotation of then-Cardinal Joseph Ratzinger given at the head of this chapter, Ratzinger wrote metaphorically of a "glass" wall between those already in eternal life and earth-living members of the Church. It is surely a "permeable wall" that separates earth-dwellers from heaven-dwellers in the Communion of Saints. The tremendous possibilities of relationship within the reality of the whole Church depend on faith and a humble openness to the ways in which God desires to encounter us,

---

[186] Eucharistic Prayer I, "The Order of Mass," in *Breaking Bread: With Daily Mass Propers, 2016* (Portland, Oregon: John J. Limb Pub., 2015), 17.

including communications and assistance offered through angels, saints, and those whose final purification we remember in prayer. The experiences of the first days of the Church, recalled earlier in this chapter, have never been declared a closed privileged time.

Each year the Church celebrates the Feast of All Saints on November 1, followed by the Feast of All Souls. Unfortunately, these feasts have mainly become the occasion of secular, gross, even obscene caricatures of the mysteries of the Communion of Saints. In addition, there are both serious and inane misunderstandings concerning the means of requesting the intercession of saints. Magic and sorcery aside, excesses in the veneration of saints can make idols of them to the neglect of the Eucharist and the sacramental life of faith.

The reality of wholesome relationships with the saints and those undergoing a final purgation can follow liturgical prayer with a simple loving directness of communication as was evident in the Acts of the Apostles, and indeed the Gospels. Jesus led by example; He directly addressed His Father (and ours) as "Abba," or "Daddy."

Our Lady's appearances, though usually suffused with light, are attractively amazing but not fearful. Her officially recognized apparitions have been given mainly to young (mostly poor) children, or adults in unprivileged circumstances. When describing who had appeared to them, the seers have referred to the Blessed Mother as a

"Lady" or a "beautiful Lady." The Mother of God speaks to those whom she surprises in their own language, and in settings familiar to them: a cove by the small French River Gave in the case of Bernadette of Lourdes; a small holm oak tree for the children of Fatima; a mountain path to Juan Diego in Mexico. Some have not only seen Our Lady, but have experienced her touch. Juan Diego said that the Mother of God arranged the roses in his tilma with Her own hands. The young postulant Catherine, at Rue de Bac in Paris, was awakened by a young child who led her to the chapel which was "lit up" as for a Midnight Mass. Catherine heard a rustling sound at the approach of the Mother of God, and knelt beside Her in the convent sanctuary.

Even before Mary appeared to the shepherd children of Fatima, they were visited by an angel who approached them in light above the field where they were watching sheep, but also knelt with them in prayer. Though surrounded by light, the angel had the appearance of a youth. He taught the children (all less than ten years of age) how to pray and sacrifice simply. On his last visit to them, the angel, who identified himself as the Angel of Portugal, gave them their First Communion from a chalice which, at first, was suspended in the air.

Later, when Our Lady came, she entrusted the "secrets of Fatima" to these children and promised that she would show a great sign on October 13, 1917. An estimated crowd of 70,000 gathered in the area of Cova de Iria on that day and witnessed the "Miracle of the Sun" as the Mother of God lifted her hand toward the sun, and it spun and bathed a large area of the countryside in changing colors. An unprecedented sun event occurred at the mere gesture of Mary. The sun spun, careened toward earth and back again. In reading accounts of the Church-approved apparitions of Our Lady, one is struck by the ordinary details that are associated with those heavenly visits, the way they fit into the local time and circumstances, and yet show a "divine penchant" for surprise, for unexpected Marian requests, and for the concern of the Mother of God regarding dangers and violence that would be inflicted upon a pope, the Church, specific nations, and the entire world. Mary comes at times of particular restlessness in the world, or in anticipation of them.

When members of our family or friends die, how significant it is that the relationships with them continue and deepen, and their ongoing assistance be welcomed. It may be as simple as the realization of their presence, or of speaking to them silently or aloud. St. Teresa of Avila and other saints have shared their experiences of conversing with family members and friends who have died. Teresa, for example, spoke of relating to her friend, Peter of Alcantara, after his death. Therese of Lisieux's familiar promise that she would spend her eternity doing good on earth is attested to by many who have been assisted and/ or consoled by her.

When I was a child, we lived on a farm in southern Minnesota during years of drought and poverty. An elderly deaf woman named Mary Marek lived about a mile away. Occasionally, she would walk across the fields to visit my mother who would write out responses to Mary's sharing and questions. One day before she left, Mary stood in the bleak yard between the barn and the house and said to my mother, "Someday there will be a religious house here." At the time it made no sense. My mother remembered it some forty-three years later when the vacated animal barn was renovated into a house and women religious came to live on the land, where Mass is now celebrated daily in a simple chapel. So much depends upon the restlessness of the human heart that makes it open to the coming and going not only of electrons, light waves and the pull of gravity, but relationships that move between the seen and the unseen, between those on pilgrimage and those who already are in eternal life.

Angels, so readily recognized in the Scriptures as powerful messengers of God, are often thought of as imaginary chubby babes with wings. Such images are found on greeting cards, paintings, and sculptures. The mighty messengers of God are then reduced in common understanding to innocuous, whimsical images.

A Rabbi in Canada told simply of a happening on a lonely Saskatchewan road. He spoke of a night when he and his wife were driving home on a two-lane road. They realized that an approaching car was veering toward their headlights. There was nowhere to turn. The car, seemingly driven by an intoxicant, came upon them, but lifted up and drove right above them and continued on its way. The Rabbi spoke softly of the event, and was telling of celestial protection. How many times in our lives have we been visited by saints and angels and have not been aware?

At the Last Supper, Christ spoke of heaven. He said, "Let not your hearts be troubled; believe in God, believe also in me. In my Father's house are many rooms; if it were not so, would I have told you that I go to prepare a place for you? And when I go and prepare a place for you, I will come again and will take you to myself, that where I am you may be also." (Jn 14: 1-3). No wonder our hearts are restless for that fulfillment.

Chapter VII

TRINITARIAN LIFE: PERICHORETIC SELF-GIFT

Divine communion means the capacity to go out and to remain at the same 'time.' Each person is necessarily within the other two, and yet is simultaneously an irresistible outward impulse into the other two. There is an 'unceasing circulation of life.'[187]

Long before the twentieth century penchant for motion and process, Cyril of Alexandria described Trinitarian relations as 'reciprocal irruption'..... English words suggesting perichoretic union are 'dancing about,' 'encompassing,' 'coinhering,' and 'interpenetrating.'[188]

---

[187] See A. M. Bermejo, "Circumincession," *New Catholic Encyclopedia* Vol. III (San Francisco, 1967), 880.

[188] Mary Timothy Prokes, *Mutuality: The Human Image of Trinitarian Love* (New York: Paulist Press, 1993), 30.

eaven is described as seeing God "face-to-face." This is a profound mystery that involves the inner reality of God. At the Last Supper, Jesus told the Apostles that in His Father's house there are many rooms, and that He personally was going to prepare a place for them. (Jn 14:2) When Thomas protested that they didn't know where He was going, or the way, Jesus said "I am the way, and the truth, and the life; no one comes to the Father, but by me. If you had known me, you would have known my Father also; henceforth you know him and have seen him." (Jn 14: 6-7)

When Philip countered with "Lord, show us the Father, and we shall be satisfied," (Jn 14: 8) the Lord responded to him with questions:

> Have I been with you so long, and yet you do not know me, Philip? He who has seen me has seen the Father; how can you say, 'Show us the Father'? Do you not believe that I am in the Father and the Father in me? The words that I say to you I do not speak on my own authority; but the Father who dwells in me does his works. (Jn 14:9-10)

These were revelations of divine relationship – love words of seeing, presence, indwelling – that also touch us now. Just sixteen days before he announced his resignation from the papacy on February 11, 2013, Pope Benedict XVI gave a General Audience Address on what it means to seek the face of God. Reflecting on "Holy Christmas," and divine revelation reaching its culmination point in the Incarnation, Benedict said:

> God himself became man. Jesus does not tell us something about God, he does not merely speak of the Father but is the Revelation of God, because he is God and thus reveals the face of God. In the Prologue to his Gospel St. John wrote: 'no one has ever seen God; the only Son, who is in the bosom of the Father, he has made him known' (Jn 1:18). I would like to dwell on the phrase 'reveals God's face.'[189]

In Jesus' response to Philip "He who has seen me has seen the Father," said Benedict, there is a summing up of the New Testament: "God can be seen, God has shown his face, he is visible in Jesus Christ."[190] The Pope spoke of the "quest for God's face" that is present in the Old Testament. The Hebrew term *panim*, meaning "face"

---

[189] Pope Benedict XVI, General Audience, Jan. 16, 2013. https://www.catholicculture.org/culture/library/view.cfm?recnum=10154 (accessed Apr. 21, 2016).

[190] Pope Benedict XVI, General Audience.

recurs 400 times there, 100 of them referring to God. For the devout Israelite who knew that no image could be fashioned to portray God, "it was affirmed that God has a face – meaning he is a 'you' who can enter into relationship..... he addresses us, he listens to us, he sees us, he speaks to us, he makes a covenant, he is capable of love," and through salvation history, gradually "makes himself, his face, known."[191]

Pope Benedict briefly spoke of Moses' familiarity with God, and the saying in Exodus that "The Lord used to speak to Moses face to face, as a man speaks to his friend." (Ex 33:11) Yet, Moses was told by God that he would only "see my back, but my face shall not be seen." (Ex 33:23) Benedict explained that according to the "Fathers," it meant that although Moses conversed with God as with a friend, "see God's back" meant a *following* of Christ, and through that, Moses would see the mystery of God "from behind."[192] With the Incarnation, the search for the face of God was given an "unimaginable turning-point" – the face of God is Jesus, God become man. Moses would receive the *name* of God, but not see Jesus, God's *face* in human history. In every human person, "even in atheists," said the Pope, there is the innate desire to see God's face. This calls for the following of Christ with one's whole life. The

---

[191] Pope Benedict XVI, General Audience.

[192] Pope Benedict XVI, General Audience.

disciples from Emmaus recognized the risen Lord in the breaking of bread, and "for us too the Eucharist is the great school in which we learn to see God's face, we enter into a close relationship with him, and at the same time we learn to turn our gaze to the final moment of history when he will satisfy us with the light of his face."[193] The longing to see God face-to-face is closely linked to St. Augustine's cry that "Our hearts are restless until they rest in thee." Our "Age of Restlessness" is flooded with conflicting meanings and imagery of "seeing face to face." In competitive marketing strategies, products are blatantly associated with face-to-face contexts that often having a sexual connotation – even though the items being advertised may be automobiles, lingerie, coffee, or insurance policies. Similarly, contemporary "rock stars" and those who sing for public affairs feel obliged to express with contorted faces and bodies either 1) anguished longing to be sexually active with a beloved; or 2) desperation over a relationship "gone south." More graphically, pornography in its multiple forms degrades not only sexual organs and activity, but the meaning of the gift of sight and the wonder of a beloved's face and eyes.

Jesus, in detailed and colorful language, spoke of the Last Judgment in terms of a gathering of all humanity where each would be judged in terms of charity to one's

---

[193] Pope Benedict XVI, General Audience.

neighbor. He spoke of a separation between those who had done the works of mercy in earthly life and those who failed to do so. Both groups will be incredulous when told: "As you did it to the least of my brethren, you did it to me." Jesus was stating that it was essential to *see* and respond to the face of Christ in spouse, child, friend, immigrant, and hospice patient – as well as in a sneering persecutor, human trafficker, or murderer. He said that charity given (or withheld) will be the standard for judgment. How significant to *see* all we encounter with the gaze of Christ and to recognize the responsibility accompanying that seeing!

To gaze in this sense does not mean to look upon with curiosity, pity, lasciviousness, or even horror. It means to look at a person or thing with love in union with the merciful eyes of Christ. In some translations of Scripture, Christ's gaze is described as "looking intently" at a person. There was a deliberateness, an intentionality in the way that Christ "saw" or "looked" at a person. Mark's Gospel tells of Jesus' response to the rich young man who said that he had kept all the commandments from his youth: Jesus, "looking upon him, loved him." (Mk 10:23) Zacchaeus, head tax collector of Jericho, had climbed a tree in order to see Jesus when He would pass by. When he came beneath the tree, Jesus looked up, asked him to come down – and then invited himself to Zacchaeus' house. (Lk 19:1-10) The tax man hustled down from the tree and hosted a banquet for Jesus in his home. One day when Jesus passed by the tax office in Capernaum, He is said to have *looked* at Matthew there, and invited the tax man to follow him. Matthew responded immediately, got up from his tax booth and followed Jesus. (Matt 9:9)

Pope Francis spoke of Matthew the tax collector's conversion, when Jesus looked at him "right in the eye."

> That gaze overtook him completely, it changed his life. We say he was converted. He changed his life. As soon as he felt that gaze in his heart, he got up and followed him. This is true: Jesus' gaze always lifts us up. It is a look that always lifts us up, and never leaves you in your place, never lets us down, never humiliates. It invites you to get up – a look that brings you to grow, to move forward, that encourages you, because the One who looks upon you loves you. The gaze makes you feel that he loves you. This gives the courage to follow Him. And he got up and followed him.[194]

---

[194] Pope Francis, "Jesus' loving gaze rekindles the embers of our desire for God: Pope Francis' Homily for the Feast of St. Matthew, Evangelist," Sept. 21, 2013, Saltandlighttv.org. http://saltandlighttv. org/blog/fr-thomas-rosica/jesus-loving-gaze-rekindles-the-embers-of-our-desire-for-god-pope-francis-homily-for-the-feast-of-st-matthew-the-evangelist (accessed Apr. 22, 2016).

Anyone who has received the gaze of love, eye to eye, knows what a loving moment of truth it is. There is a sense that the one whose gaze has been received has looked into the depths within. There is at once a sense of being unworthy of the love of the gazer, and a desire to become more worthy, a desire never to lose that gaze. Peter would have known that penetrating moment when Christ looked upon him in the courtyard of the High Priest.

> And after an interval of about an hour still
> another insisted, saying 'Certainly this man
> also was with him; for he is a Galilean.' But
> Peter said, 'Man, I do not know what you are
> saying.' And immediately, while he was still
> speaking, the cock crowed. And the Lord
> turned and looked at Peter. (Lk 22:59-61)

In his commentary on this passage, Dr. Ralph F. Wilson writes that Jesus turns "and makes eye contact with Peter. The word translated 'looked straight at' (NIV) or 'looked upon' (KJV) is the Greek verb *emblepo*," means "'to look at something directly and therefore intently, 'look at, gaze on.'"[195] The gaze of Christ was the gaze of the Son of God accommodated to the flesh and blood of His human

---

[195] Dr. Ralph F. Wilson, "#101." Peter's Denial (Luke 22:54-62)," in *jesuswalk.com*, http://www.jesuswalk.com/lessons/22_54-62.htm (accessed Apr. 22, 2016).

nature. It is the touchstone of all human eye contact, person-to-person and person-to-object. The significance of looking, and of intentionally choosing who and what one will gaze at relates directly to the immense meaning of the gaze of Christ.

Much of contemporary restlessness in world-wide cultures is related to the gift of sight, its use and misuse. The human face and body have become commodities in an era when affluence and multiple instruments of convenience provide opportunities for immediate pleasure in what is portrayed visually in electronic or printed form. Whatever enters one's body-person through the eyes remains in memory, even though it may be "forgotten" for a time. How readily places, persons, events and natural occurrences (both the splendid and the horrific) can be called up in memory, or evoked unwillingly by a later sense-experience. Pope Francis underscores the blessing and the need of "remembering."

> We must look back to see how God has saved us, follow – with our hearts and minds – this path with its memories and in this way arrive at Jesus' side. It's the same Jesus, who in the greatest moments of his life – Holy Thursday and Good Friday, in the (Last) Supper – gave us his Body and Blood and said to us 'Do This in memory of me.' In

memory of Jesus. To remember how God saves us! ..... But we must memorize our past and be a memorial of our own lives and our own journey.[196]

The Holy Father was urging a way of gazing into one's past in order to acknowledge with gratitude what God has done, including the times when one has refused His presence: "And the times when I said to the Lord: No! Go away! I don't want you! Our Lord respects (our wishes.) He is respectful."[197]

SEEING FACE TO FACE

Peter, in post-Easter life, would have internalized the power of Christ's gaze so deeply that he was able to know what his own gaze could mean for others. The Acts of the Apostles relates how Peter and John were entering the Temple at the Beautiful Gate in the afternoon. A beggar called out for an alms. "And Peter directed his gaze at him, with John, and said, 'Look at us.' And he fixed his attention upon them, expecting to receive something from them. But Peter said, 'I have no silver and gold, but I give

---

[196] Pope Francis, Homily at Casa Santa Marta, Apr. 21, 2016. https://zenit.org/articles/popes-morning-homily-we-must-memorize-gods-be...(accessed Apr. 23, 2016).

[197] Pope Francis, Homily at Casa Santa Marta.

you what I have; in the name of Jesus of Nazareth, walk.'"
(Acts 3:4-6) It was an eye-to-eye moment in the name of
Jesus, and the man rose up, and began walking, leaping
and praising God.

Jim McDonnell, in assessing the meaning of "social
communities" in cyberspace, observes that names given
to social networking companies carry something of the
range of possibilities they encompass, noting, for example,
how "*Facebook* has overtones of a photo album but is also
a place where the user can choose a 'face' to present to
the world."[198] Evil can subvert what is good and precious.
When the finest of any created reality is corrupted, it is
especially vile. This is certainly true of the beauty and
awe of the gaze.

TO STARE PORNFULLY

Earlier, it was pointed out that pornography's allure
touches desires that it cannot fulfill. It *objectifies* persons
and acts which, when authentic, are intensely *intimate
and personal expressions of love and respect.* Pornography
invites the "stare" as it deconstructs, mangles and writhes
with a particular disgust, even though it may cause sexual
arousal and sensual pleasure. The beauty of the human
body and sexual communion is degraded, not only in

---

[198] Jim McDonnell, "Crossing borders in virtual space," *Media
Development* 4/2009, 6.

those who use it perversely; it also degrades those who either willingly or through coercion portray it. *Time* magazine's cover story "Porn and the Threat to Virility" by Belinda Luscombe raised frank concerns about the effects of pornography in the lives of the young. Both religious and secular commentators quote a major statement of the *Time article:*

> A growing number of young men are convinced that their sexual responses have been sabotaged because their brains were virtually marinated in porn when they were adolescents. Their generation has consumed explicit content in quantities and varieties never before possible, on devices designed to deliver content swiftly and privately, all at an age when their brains were more plastic – more prone to permanent change – than in later life. These young men feel like unwitting guinea pigs in a largely unmonitored decade-long experiment in sexual conditioning.[199]

The article by Luscombe dwells particularly on the way in which saturation in pornography has affected the

---

[199] Belinda Luscombe, "Porn and the Threat to Virility," *Time*, Vol.187, No.13, 42.

capacity of young men to relate with real women. It is regrettable that the landmark secular article on the devastation of pornography focused only on males. That it raises the complex of deadly consequences of pornography however, is important. Commentator Denny Burk notes that while the article provided a "rational look" at the use of modern porn among males, "it seems unaware that it is narrating a civilizational crisis."[200] He saw that the article is evidence of a diminishing ability to talk about sex in moral terms. "We are at a place in our culture in which sexual morality has been reduced to consent. Our society has embraced total sexual license." Even after narrating the "devastating consequence of porn use," says Burk, the article "cannot bring itself to condemn pornography as a moral evil."[201] The magnitude of pornographic infiltration is both a contributory factor and patent sign of civilizational crisis.

Created in the image and likeness of God, human persons are made for interpersonal communion, for enduring intercourse on many levels that express an exchange of personal self-gift. "Sexuality is our human capacity as whole persons to enter into love-giving, life-giving union

---

[200] Denny Burke, "The Darkness of Porn and the Hope of the Gospel," *Christian Culture*, Apr. 4, 2016, http://www.dennyburk.com/the-darkness-of-porn-and-the-hope-of-the-gospel/ (accessed Apr. 24, 2016).

[201] Burke, "The Darkness of Porn."

in and through the body in ways that are appropriate."[202] Being an exchange of personal self-gift, human sexuality is not confined to certain bodily organs or acts. It is a *human* capacity: only embodied persons can be sexual in this manner. Being created in divine image, but *embodied* as male and female, woman and man are fulfilled not only in mutual self-gift to one another, but in being "fruitful," in bringing their combined self-gifts to another: giving life to a child, assistance to their neighbor, and reverence to the good creation entrusted to their stewardship.

The "Age of Restlessness" is marked by a feverish desire to abolish all boundaries in order to achieve freedom and fulfillment. In terms of sexuality, this means understanding love-giving, life-giving self-gift as a set of legal barriers to be abolished, or simply ignored. As the article by Belinda Lipscombe shouted an alarm in the public square, however, there is sudden panic among young men that after *living without barriers*, there is the realization that they have been "done-to." They have even lost their capacity/desire for natural sexual intercourse with real women. As Burk noted, the men willing to sound this alarm are more concerned about losing their capacity for physical expression of intercourse than having lost the meaning of sexuality. One of the men interviewed for the article said that he would "tell my son" that there are side

---

[202] Mary Timothy Prokes, *Toward a Theology of the Body"* (Grand Rapids, Michigan: William B. Eerdmans Publishing Co, 1996), p. 95.

effects of pornography, that "all superstimulating things, like Internet porn, junk food and drugs, can be fun and pleasurable temporarily.....However, they also have the potential to desensitize you to normal, natural things and ultimately rob you of the one thing you thought they would give you, the ability to experience pleasure."[203]

There should be no surprise that the "restless hearts" of persons and entire cultures have become frantic in search of fulfillment and peace. Made for God, made in the likeness of God, the human heart searches for the mystery of Love. In his First Letter, St. John wrote: "Beloved, let us love one another; for love is of God, and he who loves is born of God and knows God. He who does not love does not know God; for God is love." (I Jn 4:7-8)

To ascertain what is able to fulfill heart-deep restlessness, that of which Augustine cried out, "Our hearts are made toward you, O God, and they are restless until they rest in you," it is necessary to ask again and again: Who is God? Who is like God? Augustine and Bonaventure wrote of the "vestiges" of the Creator in creation. Synonyms of "vestiges" that seem particularly apt in speaking of vestiges of God in relation to creation are fingerprints or footprints, signs, indications, glimmer, or "the visible" left by Someone. All are inadequate to convey the depth of what can be known of the reality because the Creator has not

---

[203] Luscombe, "Porn and the Threat to Virility," 47.

left the ongoing work of Creation. The "fingerprints" or "reminders" recall experiences of personal living encounters rather than cold reminders of a distant potentate who has gone away after bestowing a gracious benevolence.

Shortly after he was elected pope, in a homily at Domus Santae Marthae, Pope Francis spoke about the mistaken idea that many have of God. While they profess belief in God, the Pope said, in what kind of God do they believe? God is real, "not some intangible essence or esoteric mist like 'god-spray.'" It was a simile that he would repeat in other homilies in speaking of God. From the initial period of his papacy, Francis built upon his predecessor's emphasis on *encounter with the living God*:

> We believe in God who is Father, who is Son, who is Holy Spirit..... We believe in persons and when we talk to God we speak with persons who are concrete and tangible, not some misty, diffused god-like 'god-spray,' that's a bit everywhere but who knows what it is.[204]

To grapple with what it will mean to see God "face-to-face" in heaven, then, involves the realization that we

---

[204] Pope Francis, Homily at Domus Sanctae Marthae, Apr. 18, 2013, in "Pope: God is real, concrete person, not mysterious intangible mist," http://www.catholicnews.com/services/englishnews/2013/pope-god-is-real (accessed Apr. 25, 2016).

believe in a God who has already come in our flesh and presented a human face. Even after His thirty-three years of saving presence His face was mocked, spit upon, and terribly wounded. In longing for sight of "God's face" in eternal life there is first the need to ponder how we recognize and respond to *Jesus'* face and what His face meant in Nazareth and Jerusalem in his earthly presence – and what it means to recognize the face of Christ in the human persons we encounter daily – and what it means to see the ghastly caricature of human love in pornography. More important than asking what the human body will "look like" in eternal life, is the need to ponder and pray about what it will mean to see the Face of God in eternal life. In the Gospel of John, Jesus' prayer to the Father and his dialogue with the Apostles revealed the inner life of the Trinity not as an abstraction, nor as a vague presence, but as an active, total self-gift among Father, Son and Holy Spirit. Divine Persons *want* to indwell us as They are and as we are. Consider what John records of Christ's Trinitarian revelation in the Upper Room, where He spoke to His apostles of His self-gift in Body and Blood. He was revealing what it means that *the God of their entire Hebrew history is the intensely vibrant relationship of Father, Son and Holy Spirit.*

The Apostles knew in at least an elementary way that Abraham in his humanity had experienced God. The Apostles also knew something of Moses who encountered

God on sacred ground at the burning bush, and that he asked the name of God and received the full-of-divine-mystery answer: "I AM who I AM." How intensely close they were to the One who identified Himself as "I AM." Earlier, it was noted how significant it was for Jesus during the years of His public life to identify with "I am": 1) "I am the bread of life" (Jn 6:35; 2) "I am the light of the world" (Jn 8:12); 3) "I am the gate" (Jn 10:9); 4) "I am the good shepherd" (Jn 10:11); 5) "I am the resurrection and the life" (Jn 11:25); 6) ""I am the way, and the truth, and the life" (Jn 14:6); and 7) "I am the true vine." (Jn 15:1)

There is a further "I AM" reference that is of great importance in John's Gospel. It is not followed by a metaphoric term such as light, or gate, or bread. It is the straightforward statement of personal existence given in John 8:58 where Jesus responded to those who were accosting Him in the Temple and accusing Him of having a demon: "Before Abraham was, I AM." (Jn 8:58).

Some Biblical scholars who study the name of God as revealed to Moses have found that there is evidence for claiming that the meaning of the mysterious "I AM" (known also as the Tetragrammaton) bears also a sense of being a faithful presence. Michael Whelan, for example, says: "Given that the Lord is revealed as 'I AM WHO AM' – see Exodus 3:14 – the promise to be with us is a promise of Mystery Presence. 'I shall be there as who I am shall I be there.'"[205]

At the Last Supper, in the final evening of his earthly life with His Apostles, Jesus explicitly and tenderly spoke of the inner life of God and what this meant for them. Jesus prayed (spoke) intimately to the Father in the presence of those about to witness His capture and Passion. In answering their anxious and uncomprehending queries about where He was going, Jesus assures the Apostles: "If a man loves me, he will keep my word, and my Father will love him, and we will come to him and make our home with him." (Jn 14:23) Jesus asked Philip: "Do you not believe that I am in the Father and the Father in me? The words that I say to you I do not speak on my own authority; but the Father who dwells in me does his works." (Jn 14:10) It was revelation given as never heard before. If the Apostles were to *know* a human entry into Trinitarian relationships, they were to keep Jesus' commandments of love. To "know" was not an objective knowledge of abstruse facts. It was deeply personal:

> If you love me you will keep my commandments. And I will pray the Father, and he

---

[205] Michael Whelan, "Gospel for Second Sunday of Advent (6 December 2015)," http://.aquinas-academy.com/gospel-notes/498-gospel-for-second-sunday-of-Advent-6-december-2015 (accessed Apr. 25, 2016).

will give you another Counselor, to be with you forever, even the Spirit of truth, whom the world cannot receive, because it neither sees him nor knows him; you know him, for he dwells with you, and will be in you. (Jn 14:15-17)

If a man loves me, he will keep my word, and my Father will love him, and we will come to him and make our home with him. (Jn 14:23)

Nevertheless I tell you the truth; it is to your advantage that I go away, for if I do not go away, the Counselor will not come to you; but if I go, I will send him to you..... I have yet many things to say to you, but you cannot bear them now. When the Spirit of truth comes, he will guide you into all the truth. (Jn 16:7;12-13)

Think of it humanly. Even while a mob was assembling nearby, preparing to ambush Him in the Garden of Gethsemane, Jesus Christ in an Upper Room in Jerusalem was speaking to His Father in the Holy Spirit from within the living Trinity. In the midst of a mostly uncomprehending group of Apostles, caught up in their own fears and envies, Jesus was praying and speaking experientially of His active and forever relationships within the Trinity. He *is* the eternal Son of the Father, never doing, saying or willing anything apart from Him. All that He is telling the small band of followers at the Last Supper, He is handing on in union with the Holy Spirit. It was the Face of God made known in explicit terms to those who could receive it in a beginning way.

One of the great gifts of twentieth century theology was a fresh pondering of the relationships within the Blessed Trinity, and how the inner life of God illumines the meaning of human life and relationships.

Jean Danielou explained that for Christians, spiritual life consists in being led into the sphere of the Trinity. The mystery that has been revealed to us, says Danielou, is "God's human visage." Danielou prayerfully wrote of seeing the Face of God in terms of each person of the Blessed Trinity:

> The life of the Trinity reveals the Father's face to us in the particular relationship we have formed with Him through grace.....
> At the same time it is through the Son that another aspect of God's human face is revealed to us. This is God's communication of Himself, His eternal fertility, the manner in which the life that is within Him is at the same time totally given and totally

received in the Son. And in His turn the Holy
Spirit also gives expression to God's human
face since it is the personal statement of the
mutual love of the Father and the Son.[206]

The whole basis of *being*, said Danielou, is community
of persons. The Trinitarian mystery illuminates human
situations and teaches that the very basis of the existence
and the *real* is "love in the sense of community of persons."[207] There is a certain exuberance in Danielou's discussion of *communion* as the basis of being. The entire
foundation of Christian revelation rests on the Trinity.
In the final analysis, says Danielou, "all reality can be
summed up in the phrase: 'Let them be one as we are one.'
This means two things. 'We are one:' these simple words
flash out with a blinding light. Not only do they say that
there is a 'we' and a 'one,' but that the one *is* a we. The one
is a we: nobody, before Christ, had said this! The One, that
is the Absolute, is a We. The One is a communion among
the Three. The One is an eternal exchange of love."[208]

It took a long time to reconcile what Jesus revealed
of inner Trinitarian life with the monotheism of the Old
Testament that had to stress with great rigor among pagan

---

[206] Jean Danielou, *God's Life in Us*, trans Jeremy Leggat (Denville, New
Jersey: Dimension Books, 1969), 44.

[207] Danielou, *God's Life in Us*, 45.

[208] Danielou, *God's Life in Us*, 46.

nations who worshipped their multiple "gods" that there is only One God, and none other. It took several centuries of reflection, prayer, and labor on the part of the early Church to articulate the revealed mystery in the most suitable way possible in the Greek and Latin languages. Richard Schneider says: "The reconciliation of the absolute unity in God with the threefold personal distinction was reached above all in Western theology. The unity rests in the divine nature and substance, and the distinction is seen only in terms of the relations of the three persons to one another."[209]

What Jesus revealed to the Apostles in human words concerning the inner life of God was spoken in the Mediterranean-rim languages of the time. It needed to be handed on and explicated for ensuing generations, cultures and language groups in ways that convey the truth of this revelation without distortion. Jesus revealed what is of deepest mystery, what is of divine love, what divine persons forever mutually express in self-gift. This cannot be described adequately in even the most precise philosophical or theological terms. While no word or phrase will be a total way of passing on from age to age what has been revealed of God's inner life and divine identity, one of the most helpful terms chosen by theologians is the Greek word *perichoresis*.

---

[209] Richard Schneider, "The Human Person as the Image of the Three-Personal God," lecture, Marquette University, Milwaukee, Wisconsin, Aug. 8, 1966.

Leonardo Boff explains why it is an apt term because it expresses complementary aspects of Trinitarian relationship: an indwelling, and a going-out. When *perichoresis* is translated into Latin, it requires two words to articulate the twofold meaning. Boff's explanation shows why these words are so helpful when describing relations among Father, Son and Holy Spirit, as Jesus revealed them in his intimate prayer to the Father and His final discourse to the Apostles at the Last Supper:

> Theology came to use the Greek word *perichoresis* to express the interpenetration of one Person by the others..... Its first meaning is that of being contained in another, dwelling in, being in another – a situation of fact, a static state. This understanding was translated by *circuminsessio*, a word derived from *sedere*, and *sessio*, being seated, having its seat in, seat. Applied to the mystery of the communion of the Trinity this signified: one Person is in the others, surrounds the others on all sides (*circum-*), occupies the same space as the others, fills them with its presence. Its second meaning is active and signifies the interpenetration or interweaving of one Person with the others and in the others. This

understanding seeks to express the living and eternal process of relating intrinsic to the three Persons, so that each is always penetrating the others. This meaning was translated as *circumincessio*, derived from *incedere*, meaning to permeate, com-penetrate and interpenetrate.[210]

The inner life of God is love totally, forever given. It is the relation of each to the others in personal self-gift. Nothing that one Person is or does is apart from the others. The Personal identification of Father, Son, and Holy Spirit is in their *relationships* with one another. In the Creed, belief is professed in one Lord, Jesus Christ, eternally begotten of the Father, and consubstantial with the Father. He is *begotten, not made*, and through Him all things were made. We also profess belief in the Holy Spirit, the giver of life, who *proceeds* from the Father and the Son. In the perichoretic love communion of the Trinity, there is a divine dynamism that is creative and life-giving – *restless*.

Theologian Richard Schneider pointed out that part of a believer's difficulty in receiving and responding to the reality of God's inner life stems from the way that for many centuries Trinitarian theology strongly focused on the divine *nature* rather than on the interpersonal

---

[210] Leonardo Boff, *Trinity and Society* (Maryknoll, New York, 1988), 135-136.

relationships among divine Persons. This is significant because human beings are not created as images of divine *nature*, but of divine *Persons*. The truth about God that Jesus lived and revealed with greatest emphasis was the relationships among the Father, Son and Holy Spirit. While there is need to *know* the characteristics of the divine nature, humans are not made in the image of that divine *nature* – but of divine persons who are identified by their interpersonal *relationships*.

Two things followed from this misplaced emphasis, said Schneider. First, the more that a believer reflects on the three-personal God, "the more he lives, realizes – in the full sense of the word – his personhood."[211] Second, "a more adequate understanding of the revelation of the three-personal God, as taken place in Christ, will help the Christian to know more correctly himself, what he is called to be, what he is created to be, namely the image of the divine person."[212]

The essential characteristics of a person, said Schneider, are immanence and transcendence. *Immanence* is the ability to realize one's distinctness, one's difference from every other being. It signifies the self as a center of responsibility. *Transcendence*, on the other hand, allows one to move beyond self, to penetrate into the rest of reality and organize one's perspective in three directions: to the community, the

---

[211] Schneider, "The Human Person in the Divine Image."

[212] Schneider, "The Human Person in the Image."

world, and God. What is vital here is knowing that the imma-
nent knowing of oneself is *realized* in transcending oneself
in relationships. Accordingly, a person becomes more himself in the measure in which he relates himself, Schneider
emphasized. Within one divine nature, the Trinity is united.

> Because of this unity, the Father is entirely
> in the Son and entirely in the Holy Spirit; the
> Son is entirely in the Father and entirely in
> the Holy Spirit; the Holy Spirit is entirely in
> the Father and entirely in the Son. In tech-
> nical terms, in the understanding of Western
> theology the divine persons are subsistent
> relations; which means nothing else than that
> the divine persons fulfil the ideal synthesis
> between immanence and transcendence.[213]

God is not an aloof abstraction but the
eternal three-personal center of love. Out of
the chaotic mid-twentieth century, Henri de
Lubac wrote:

> If man wants to find himself, he must
> aim above and beyond himself.....It is not
> enough for each individual to take on a task

---

[213] Schneider, "The Human Person in the Image."

that transcends him; the same must be true
of each generation and for each community, and in fact for humanity as a whole.....
Humanity can only find equilibrium and
peace – an active peace, equilibrium in
movement – by keeping its gaze fixed above
the earthly horizon, in being faithful to its
divine vocation.[214]

The introductory quotation at the head of this chapter
cites Cyril of Alexandria (Patriarch of Alexandria in the
fifth century) who described Trinitarian relations as a
"reciprocal irruption." That is a term from Christianity's
fifth century, from a doctor of the Church who emphasized
relationships within the Trinity that are vibrant and active.
Cyril served as Patriarch of Alexandria, Egypt, in a time
that also was filled with chaos, terror, and strong theological debate that shook the Eastern Church and led to the
Council of Ephesus in 431 and the dogmatic definition of
Mary as *Theotokos*, "Mother of God." The early centuries of
the Church, following the death of the last Apostle, were
often times of struggle and intense debate regarding the
very basics of faith. Yet, the vigorous debate led to clarifica-
tions, guided by the Holy Spirit regarding authentic understanding of Trinitarian, Christological and Marian truths.

---

[214] Henri de Lubac, trans Alexander Dru, *The Discovery of God* (London:
Darton, Longman, & Todd LTD, 1960), 183-184.

In ensuing centuries, theological reflection on all aspects of faith, reached a high point in the thirteenth century. But, in regard to Trinitarian life, it would be the post-Enlightenment time, especially the mid and later twentieth century, when fresh, insightful study would shed new light on the revelation of Jesus concerning inter-personal divine life. This was enabled partly as well by the focus on, and deeper understanding of "the person" in other disciplines such as psychology, anthropology, philosophy and history.

As shown in the sequence of chapters of this book, there is a positive restlessness that characterizes all that exists. It is a *gift*. Not only is it a characteristic of the human heart, but of the whole creation in which the "vestiges" of the Creator are apparent in profusion. Poets and mystics, as well as scientists try to articulate the thirst for further fulfillment.

Theologian Henri de Lubac in *The Discovery of God* says that people can convince themselves that "metaphysical anxiety" is a thing of the past. They tell us that they have been cured of a folly for "obsession with God, with being and nothingness, of the searing burn of the unknown in the heart of the known, and of the *other* whom we pursued in our dreams."[215] People can think, said de Lubac, that they have achieved freedom in a terrible abdica-

---

[215] Henri de Lubac, *The Discovery of God*, 174.

tion. But even in them, the wretched mutilation of the greatest realities is not a finality. There may be a sudden awakening that "can relight the fire that seemed to have died out." When it *seems* that the metaphysical anxiety for God, for the "unknown in the heart of the known" has been quenched, it comes to life again. Then, says de Lubac, one can realize "the terror that he bears within him." He quotes the French poet Paul Claudel who describes the gift of restlessness that will not be satisfied by what will *never satisfy* through the analogy of a virgin mare instinctively catching a whiff of the *real thing:*

Not like a satisfied cow ruminating on its feet,

But like the virgin mare, its mouth still burning from the salt it has taken from the master's hand,

How can he keep back and restrain that huge and terrible thing that rears and cries out in the narrow stall of its personal will,

When the smell of the grass comes in through the cracks in the door with the wind at dawn? [216]

---

[216] Paul Claudel, *La Ville,* second version, Act III (1911 ed.), 291.

Theologian Henri de Lubac turns to poetry in the intensity of what he wishes to convey. The human person is wounded and when the wound breaks through the surface of consciousness "It becomes the source of a continual unrest, of a deep dissatisfaction which not only prevents the sufferer from being content with any one position, but from being satisfied with progress in any single direction."[217] Although de Lubac was writing in the past century, his words sting with the reality of all that does not bring active rest: pornographic addiction, increasing suicides, commerce involving the bodies of aborted children, and absorption in non-existent virtual worlds inhabited by avatars.

Over and over, political figures promise to work for genuine peace, even as technical instruments of war and destruction are fashioned to make them more lethal and larger in their range of destruction. The Community of believers across the world prays for peace and yet never in any previous time in history has there been such a universal destruction of human peace. Fear, the antithesis of tranquility, characterizes the state of whole races and nations. In hazardous boat trips, through night flights across national borders, uncounted numbers of people seek escape from starvation, murder, rape, human trafficking and the blade slashed across the throat. Peace is

---

[217] *The Discovery of God*, 174-175.

not the dull silence after genocide nor the horrid stillness of a prison cell. I once heard world planner Buckminster Fuller soberly comment in a lecture: "When we don't know how to solve a problem, we kill."

Genesis' elegant presentation of God's creation of the universe, states that after the dynamic "days" of creation, on the seventh day, seeing how good it all was, God "rested." The words peace and rest have a quiet, tranquil sound. Even when spoken, they give a sense of rightness, of harmony. There can be a tendency to think of peace and restfulness as a halting of activity, a cessation of noise or irritant motion. If sense stimulation softens or "stops," however, is that peace, rest?

We plant seeds, dropping or nudging them into what is often dark, perhaps odorous manured soil, and soak them with water. Then we cover them into darkness, leave them isolated. Everything seems to stop, just as the caterpillar within the butterfly cocoon seems lifeless. In either case, if the dynamic process *does stop permanently, there is a seemingly peaceful end but no new life.* If, however, despite repugnant surroundings, a seed or caterpillar continues its dramatic transformation in darkness, there will be a breakthrough. What *seemed* an ending transforms into new life. In silence, much movement is taking place in the seed that dies and then breaks open, integrating the dark soil. In turn, soil is drawn up into a fragile plant that pierces the surface of earth and rises as vibrant green, blue or yellow blades and blossoms that delight and burgeon.

We "plant" the loved bodies of those who have died. As Scripture says, in our eyes they seemed to die, but they are alive as never before – and will be (we know not how) transformed in a "new heaven and a new earth" beyond our knowing.

Peace and rest are the joy of rightness, of honest relationship, of what transcends self and is fulfilled partially on this earth in total self-gift to others. Peace and rest are not achieved through headlong plunges into the futile breaking of all boundaries, or the conquering of all frontiers to become an idol replacing God. That has been tried since Eden and ends in chaos, degradation, and hellish debauchery.

"Give us peace" is a prayer for active, creative accord with what traditionally is summed up by "the good, the true, and the beautiful." The human body "at rest" can resonate – actively but tranquilly – with a symphonic "Adagio," with a *pas de deux* exquisitely danced, with cottonwood leaves rustling in the heat of an August night, or a loon's call across a lake at dawn. These speak of peace and tranquility not because all movement has stopped, but precisely because there is a dynamism in them that accords with the inner depths of the listener, with layer upon layer of reality to the depths of earth and the myriad forms of matter that move at increasing speeds farther into outer space. It is not for nothing that the human heart is created to enter the rhythmic universe of waves, spins, and beats that reverberate through the symphony of the universe. It is the divine mystery echoed everywhere: to be, in Eliot's words, "still and still moving."

Ultimately, all of the created universe has its restlessness centered in the forever-love of the Blessed Trinity. Henri de Lubac wrote, "Humanity can only find equilibrium and peace – an active peace, equilibrium in movement – by keeping its gaze fixed above the earthly horizon, in being faithful to its divine vocation:

> "Man needs a beyond which can never be grasped, a beyond that always remains beyond. He cannot find himself without losing himself. At each stage, the final solution of the human problem lies in adoration. It can only be found in ecstasy.[218]"

---

[218] Henri de Lubac, *The Discovery of God*, 184.

CPSIA information can be obtained at www.ICGtesting.com
Printed in the USA
LVOW08s2059141016

508840LV00001B/2/P